Reading List
 Mrs. Gaskell - *Mary Barton*
 Thompson - *The Making of the English Working Class*
 G.M. Trevelyan - *English Social History*
 Halevy - *A History of the English People in 1815*

POVERTY, REVOLUTION AND THE CHURCH

International Review of Missions

POVERTY, REVOLUTION AND THE CHURCH

by

MICHAEL PAGET-WILKES

Vicar of St James, New Cross

with a Preface by

ARCHBISHOP TREVOR HUDDLESTON C.R.

EXETER
THE PATERNOSTER PRESS

ISBN 0 85364 285 0

Copyright © 1981 Michael Paget-Wilkes

All Rights Reserved. No part of this publication may be reproduced, stored in a retrieval system, or transmitted, in any form or by any means, electronic, mechanical, photocopying, recording or otherwise, without the prior permission of
THE PATERNOSTER PRESS

AUSTRALIA:
*Bookhouse Australia Ltd.,
3–7 Richmond Road, Homebush West, NSW 2140*

SOUTH AFRICA:
*Oxford University Press,
P.O. Box 1141, Cape Town*

This book is sold subject to the condition that it shall not, by way of trade or otherwise, be lent, re-sold, hired out, or otherwise circulated without the publisher's prior consent in any form of binding or cover other than that in which it is published and without a similar condition including this condition being imposed on the subsequent purchaser.

British Library Cataloguing in Publication Data
Paget-Wilkes, Michael
  Poverty, revolution and the Church.
  1. Church and social problems – Great Britain
  2. Cities and towns – Great Britain
  I. Title
  261.1′0941   HN39.G7
  ISBN 0–85364–285–0

Typeset and Printed in Great Britain for the Paternoster Press, Paternoster House, 3 Mount Radford Crescent, Exeter, Devon by Butler & Tanner Ltd., Frome, Somerset.

To John who showed me the Path.

To Gillian who guides me and walks with me along it.

Contents

Preface *by Archbishop Trevor Huddleston C.R.*	3
Prologue	5
1 Poverty and Wealth in Our Present Society . . .	9
2 The Church, the Status Quo and Inequality in the Present Day	27
3 The Church, the Elite and Poverty in History . .	50
4 Biblical Attitudes Towards the Poor and Oppressed .	67
5 Biblical Attitudes Towards Ownership and Possessions	81
6 Where do we go from here?.	96
7 The Meaning of Salvation and the Identity of the Church.	126

Preface

The reason why I am writing the Preface to this book is perhaps unusual.

It is not only that I have known Michael Paget-Wilkes for many years; it is that we have a shared experience in two of the areas which have been the background to all that he has to say. Moreover these two areas are, for those who live in them and for the rest of humanity who may prefer to ignore them, crucial to the understanding of our world. They are therefore crucial also to the understanding of the Church's mission to our world.

The process of urbanisation is now a global issue affecting the whole of humanity. At the heart of this process lies what is today known as the problem of the Inner City: and the core of that problem is deprivation, powerlessness and poverty. Its most obvious able in the cities of England: not least in London.

The other global issue of our times is the existence of what is known as The Third World: that vast segment of the human family in Africa, Asia and Latin America where, again, the core of the problem is deprivation, powerlessness and poverty. Its most obvious outward signs being over-population, hunger and death. Both in the Inner City and in the Third World the Christian Church is present and has been active at many levels of involvement over decades.

Michael Paget-Wilkes came to work on the Rondo plateau in my old diocese of Masasi, Tanzania, and had first-hand experience at grass-roots level of a typical Third World situation.

And he had that experience at a time when President Nyerere and his government were at the beginning of their experiment in African socialism. It was an exciting and stimulating time to be there and it certainly posed a massive challenge to the Christian Church. Soon after I returned from Tanzania to Stepney in 1968 Michael was working across the river in Wandsworth, in an inner city parish very similar to many of the parishes in my area. For both of us this was a time of adjustment and exploration. For both of us the issue was that of the relevance of the Church to a society which, since the Industrial Revolution, had been alienated from it and yet was the object of its pastoral concern and its mission.

This book, as the author himself says, is the direct result of his own experience as a Christian priest and evangelist. It is a courageous book, for it attempts to meet head-on the urgent questions confronting the Church in our day, and meeting them in the context of revolutionary social change. It is a book which challenges complacency, that besetting sin of middle-class Anglican Christianity. The argument is tough and draws on many sources, biblical, ideological, sociological for its support. The reader is not asked to agree with all that is written, but he can hardly fail to respond to it by asking himself further questions.

It would be a good thing for any parish or congregation if this book could become a basis for group discussion and self-examination, for, as the writer himself says:

"I have written up my search therefore as a *sharing* with those who are part of Christ's Body in the inner city, and as a *challenge* to that part of Christ's Body who live and exist in more affluent areas."

I hope both that sharing and the challenge will lead to a wide readership and I pray that God may bless the awakening which must surely follow.

TREVOR HUDDLESTON C.R.

15th October 1980

Prologue

The writing of this book began simply enough. As a minister to a church in inner London I am involved in a church life that is struggling to survive. Certain factors have appeared making the life and growth of the Church extraordinarily difficult. Questions have arisen that have no easy answers. Why is the church not growing? Why do people on their doorstep not want to know about Christ's church? Why is there such silent antagonism and fear of getting too involved? Why is the church not touching the lives of teenagers, of families, of men, of leaders, in the inner city? Why is it so rarely a true reflection of the indigenous population of the area? Why is the leadership of the church untypical and often out of touch with the area? Why is the church in the inner city conducting its own elaborate funeral service without even realising it? The questions didn't seem to be peculiar to one church, but were present in all inner city church life. But to find the answers to those questions became extraordinarily difficult. The results of the problems were plain enough but the causes were not.

Without my realising it my search led me far beyond the church life where I began. It led me to the poverty, injustice and inequality experienced by the people with whom I lived, which contrasted so markedly from the affluent lives lived by others (including myself). It led me to recognise the lack of choice and freedom available to those who 'have not' and the reality of one law for the rich and another for the poor. It led me to question the effectiveness of Socialist policies to combat such deep seated poverty and inequality (and be appalled by capitalist attitudes to poverty and inequality implemented since the writing of this book). Awareness of these facts led on to the church's position with regard to wealth, and it began to dawn on me how closely the wealthy and the church had worked for such a long time. No wonder the working class man is so hesitant to believe or accept anything to do with it. In the main it would appear that he does not believe the church (and therefore Christ) is on his side.

This led me on in turn to the fields of economics, history and theology. And I am now more than ever convinced that the life and health of the church in areas of poverty and injustice is not being decided by those churches there at present, but is being controlled mainly by structural and historical forces and by overall Christian attitudes towards poverty and injustice. Much of the despair, depression and retreat of the Christian witness in the inner city – if the truth were faced – is caused by macro issues concerning the *whole* church of which many of the membership and leadership are not even aware.

I realise that my research sometimes falls short of the expertise required for such a task, and that often I fail to live up to principles I am advocating. Yet at the same time I remain convinced that within this contradiction of Christianity (to borrow David Jenkin's book title) between Jesus' identification with the poor, the suffering, and the oppressed, and the way the church exists today, lies the heart of the matter. The failure of the church in the inner city lies within the whole church's attitude to poverty and inequality and shows how the whole church must face the issue if the contradiction is to be overcome. Only when the *corporate* body of Christ faces and responds to poverty, injustice and inequality, will the full implication of Christ's message be understood. And in facing such a major contradiction the whole church might well find a key that unlocks a new understanding of what the Christian faith is all about.

I am well aware that I have concentrated on a Christian response to poverty and inequality within the overall wealth and power distribution in England and have not touched on the massive international inequalities that exist between North and South, so well outlined in the Brandt Commission Report. Obviously many of the points of principle on the national scene are equally valid internationally and vice versa. The gap between rich and poor has an uncanny way of remaining constant at both national and international levels. The extremes may be greater internationally and these must be tackled and overcome, but that should not stop us from facing the deep seated poverty and inequality on our own doorstep at the same time.

There are different degrees of poverty eliciting different responses. Poverty is defined differently depending on one's experience or lack of experience of it. Someone from the wealthy sector of western society would see it as a lack of goods and food essential for human existence. Whereas someone who lives in poverty might rather describe it as a condition caused by the oppression of a small greedy minority. The causes of poverty also are perceived in various ways. It results from a mixture of oppression, misfortune and laziness, but while the wealthy would emphasise the third and second reasons, those who are poor would claim the first as the real cause of poverty. From my own experience, from evidence gathered by the Brandt Commission and the Royal Commission on the Distribution of Income and Wealth and from the Bible itself, I have been led to conclude that the latter view holds far greater truth. Those with first-hand experience of poverty appear to have a far deeper understanding of what poverty is and how it is caused.

Should we respond in the same way to inequality and its poverty? They are inextricably linked in that although they may sometimes exist separately, the latter accompanies and is often the result of the former, particularly when oppression, injustice and deprivation are the root causes of the inequality. If they are both caused by the oppression, selfishness and greed of the wealthy at the expense of others, then, the Christian response must be to denounce them both, regardless of the degree of poverty that results. Hence it is impossible to avoid the issue of poverty and inequality in Britain by claiming that ours is not 'real' poverty as compared to that of the third world. Dr. Sam Parmar, an Indian Christian economist, put the same issue in a different way, in a lecture given at the Free University of Amsterdam, when he said, '<u>There are no poor countries, but only countries where the conflict between the rich and the poor is greater or lesser</u>'. (quoted from C. Boerma: <u>Rich Man Poor Man and the Bible, S.C.M.</u>). Regardless of relative degree, if such inequality and poverty are maintained by oppression and deprivation then they must be rejected in the same way whether in the third world or the west.

I have written up my search therefore as a *sharing* with those who are part of Christ's body in the inner city, and as a *challenge* to that part of Christ's body who live and exist in more affluent areas. Its aim is to contribute to the opening up of the debate rather than to provide cut and dried answers.

My search has taken many years and I am most grateful to all of those who have taught me so much about life; from the Rondo plateau in Tanzania to Harper Adams Rugby club, from young people in Wandsworth to the community of a church in New Cross. I am particularly indebted to Jim Punton, John Bennington, Mike Eastman and Donald Hay who have encouraged and challenged my thinking and to Noelle Hyland and Peter Selby for their considerable editing, to Joan Crowther and Jane Bevan for all the typing that they have done, and most of all to my family who have allowed me the time to set my thoughts on paper.

CHAPTER ONE

Poverty and Wealth in Our Present Society

One of the most striking features of the world in which we live is the great gulf between rich and poor. Nobody can escape the enormity of this fact: the difference in living standards between East and West, the life expectation in India as compared with Sweden, the prosperity of Switzerland as compared with Vietnam, the wealth in Johannesburg city as compared with Soweto Township, all go to build up a picture of the massive extremes of experience that exist between those who 'have' and those who 'have not'.

At a World Conference in Lausanne in 1974 Samuel Escobar put it this way: 'Imagine that all the population of the world were condensed into one village of 100 people. In this village 67 of that 100 would be poor. The other 33 would be in varying degrees well off. Of the total population only 7 would be North Americans. The other 93 people would watch the 7 North Americans spend half of the money, eat one seventh of all the food, use half of the baths. The 7 would have 10 times more doctors than the 93. Meanwhile the 7 would continue to get more and more, and the 93 less and less.' Another way of putting the same story is by comparing the Gross National Product per person of different countries. In 1972 the per capita Gross National Product in the United States was just under £3,000 whereas in Bangladesh it was about £35 and in India about £55. In fact it has been estimated that the poorest two thirds of the world population only share a meagre 13% of the world's total Gross National Product; the other 87% is taken up by the richest third (cf. U.N. (Pearson) *Commission on International*

Development). When it comes to the ever topical matter of energy – the story is the same; North Americans consume nearly 350 times as much energy per person as compared with people who live in a country like Ethiopia (cf. *Statistical Abstract of the U.S.*, pp. 849–50).

But poverty is not confined to the Third World. It is very much present in our own country. Certainly there is a great difference between standards in the industrialised West and in the underdeveloped Third World: in that sense no one in England is really poor. Yet by the standards of our own society, with its distinctive culture and pressures, some people are in fact poor, deprived and unable to survive in our society. (There are others whose wealth is quite unimaginable to the ordinary person, for example the young man who inherited his father's dukedom and an estate of around £1,000 million – upon which, due to previous arrangements, no duty was payable!) Certainly we in England ought to respond far more responsibly to the extreme poverty of other parts of the world but we must at the same time recognise the extremes of poverty and wealth in our own society. If we fail to notice them, we are wilfully blind.

Where are the poor in Britain? They are all around us. Poverty marks certain locations. The inner cities and tower-block estates are fast becoming ghettoes of poverty. There is poverty also in rural areas and in industrial areas with high unemployment. Poverty affects specific groups of people: pensioners, one-parent families, ethnic minorities, fixed income groups and those working people who have little leverage when it comes to increasing pay awards.

Especially in big cities we may watch extremes of poverty and wealth rubbing shoulders with each other yet never meeting. They glare at each other, witnessing to the inequality at the heart of our society. This man can make a million pounds in a few days merely by lifting his telephone, returning each night in a chauffeur-driven car to his quiet, exclusive country house. But for this woman living near his office, life means spending twenty-four hours every day within earshot of three screaming children under five in a one bedroom flat, twenty-three stories up, with no husband (except Mr. Welfare State) to provide a paypacket. Our cities prove that such extremes of inequality are no dream, no fantasy – but a reality of life. For a short time, we may shield our eyes from the facts but they won't go away. If we do not live in an area of poverty we may claim that this emphasis on poverty and inequality is exaggerated. But if once we open our eyes in areas where poverty has become concentrated then we are forced to recognise that our society has a desperate problem that must be overcome.

People often imagine that poverty is simply a question of how much money a person has. But in fact, 'lack of money is only one element in a complex of deprivations which make up the experience of poverty' (J. Kincaid: *Poverty and Equality in Britain*, p. 172). Wealth does not depend simply on the number of shares or houses a person owns. Poverty and wealth have far more to do with the ability to make more out of what one possesses, utilising one's gifts and potential. As E. F. Schumacher has pointed out (in *Small is Beautiful*), wealth is intricately involved with education, discipline and organisation. The person who has been taught how to look after £1 a week, and use it most effectively, will become a millionaire far quicker than somebody who receives £10 a week but has never learned how to use or look after it. Inequality is often not just the result of different sizes of wage packets but is also related to elementary teaching about coping with life that one person receives, hence leading him to wealth and that another person does not receive, hence leading him to poverty.

Wealth is initially concerned with quantity: a wealthy person is someone who has a lot of money. But this *quantity* of wealth can also be exchanged for *quality* of life. Large quantities of wealth can buy a high material quality of existence: a large house, an attractive garden, in a quiet suburb, servants, and all the other trimmings that make life enjoyable. Poverty cannot buy that quality of life. Poverty can afford only the fumes of car exhausts, the noise of aeroplanes and trains and the sounds of the neighbours' late night party or their lavatory flushing. This difference in quality of life between wealth and poverty is another mark of inequality.

Everything we have mentioned so far lies, so to speak, on the surface of society. It is easy to be subjectively conscious of it. But fuller understanding demands that we look beneath the surface and take a more objective view. Having done so, we may consider the reasons why extremes of poverty and wealth persist.

The Presence and Persistence of Extremes of Poverty and Wealth

A visitor to Britain might easily get the impression, from public discussion and statements, that society is becoming far more balanced. Everybody seems to favour equality, everybody seeks to achieve it. Inequality, poverty and exploitation are being rapidly eliminated. Equality may not have arrived yet but it's definitely on its way.

There is a good deal to support this impression. The welfare state provides an impressive total of benefits to those who are poorly paid or deprived. Council housing is subsidised. There are unemployment benefits, health care and education are freely available for all, thus ensuring an equal start in life. Wages are increasing substantially, thanks in no small part to the extension of rights to the trades unions and their increased bargaining power. The rich, by contrast, seem to be taxed more and more so that making money seems hardly worth their while. The upper bands of income tax remain high, and the introduction of the Capital Transfer Tax has closed some of the loopholes in the old Estate Duty. Company Profits (cf. *National Income and Expenditure*, 1965–75) and the rate of return on company shares (cf. *Bank of England Quarterly Bulletin*, Vol. 16, No. 1, March 1976) have fallen considerably over the last fifteen years (though these figures tend to exaggerate the fall due to their end point being the depression year of 1974/75). Middle managers and middle class white collar workers appear to have lost some of their differentials with the unskilled and semi-skilled worker. And the wage restraint policy of the Labour government is often claimed to have helped these at the bottom rather than at the top.

It appears that there must have been a genuine reduction in the wealth of the rich and a corresponding reduction in poverty for the poor. But in fact all these developments have had little effect on the overall distribution of wealth in the country. The gap between rich and poor has scarcely been affected. Earlier reports by Professor Paish (*Lloyds Bank Review*, 1957) and Dr. Lydall (*Journal of the Royal Statistical Society*, 1959) did suggest that in post-war times the level of inequality in Britain was being reduced. But these findings have been seriously challenged ever since, particularly by Professor Titmus (*Income Distribution and Social Change*, 1962) and others (e.g. Report in *The Economist*, 15th January 1966). Indeed, as further statistics are made available and as greater experience is gained in analysing them, it is becoming increasingly clear that when measured in terms of *real* wealth, the levels of inequality, poverty and deprivation are hardly being reduced at all. 'Britain can be shown to remain a country when the concentration of wealth is still one of the highest in the world' (*New Left Review*, 1967), at one end of the scale; while at the other end poverty is still 'an endemic condition that affects a substantial part' of the population (R. Milliband, *The State and Capitalist Society*, p. 27).

Figures for the period 1960–74 given by the Royal Commission on the Distribution of Income and Wealth confirm this judgement.

1. If we look at the total wealth of the country, we find that in 1960 20% of the adult population over 18 owned 89.8% of it. By

1974 this had been reduced to 85.5% – a reduction of just over 4% in 14 years. This means that the poorest 80% increased their share by 4.3% (from 10.2% to 14.5%). (Report 4, Table 29. RCDIW Series B.)

2. When we look at changes in income for the same period we find a similar trend. In 1959 the wealthiest 10% earned 29.4% of the National Income (pre-tax). In 1974–75, they earned 26.6%, a drop of only 2.8%. And what about the poor? Whereas the poorest 50% in 1959 earned 23.1% of the national income, they had succeeded by 1974 in increasing their earnings by 1.1% to a grand total of 24.2% and if we take the years between 1967 and 1974–75, the income increase for the poorest 50% amounted to 0.1% (Report 5, Table 5, RCDIW).

These figures show that whilst there appears to be a slight change towards equality, what re-distribution has occurred is in effect a re-distribution among the wealthy. We still find that a quarter of the population owns nearly 90% of the personal wealth of the country.

Even the low figures quoted above may exaggerate the extent of re-distribution. For a high percentage of the wealth of the wealthiest is made up of company shares and securities and share prices were low in 1973–74. Figures calculated on this basis suggest that the wealthy are suffering but when their share prices increase, so does their wealth. It could also be argued that the slight trend towards the narrowing of the gap between rich and poor result mainly from the post-war increase in the number of owner occupied houses (cf. A. B. Atkinson, *The Economics of Inequality*, p. 135) rather than any significant change in genuine re-distribution.

We have already suggested that re-distribution is occurring far more 'within the classes than between them' i.e. between the very rich and the rich (cf. A. B. Atkinson, *Wealth, Income and Inequality*, 1972). The families of the rich know how to re-distribute their wealth in order to avoid tax but this does not entail movement from one sector to another. 'Ancient inequalities have assumed new and more subtle forms' (Titmus, *op. cit.* p. 119). In any case, the size of their wealth enables the wealthy to safeguard their position (see a report in *The Economist*, 15th January 1966). By seeking and using expert advice, taking judicious risks, investing in high yielding equities and leaving a minimum of their wealth in safer investments as a liquid reserve, they can ensure that 'money breeds money'. By contrast, the poorer person must needs be more careful with his limited resources and therefore cannot obtain the same level of return even from the little that he has.

Re-Distribution Policies are Ineffective

It is both remarkable and disturbing that so little has been achieved by government attempts to re-distribute wealth. Various measures have been adopted.
1. There is *direct taxation of wealth* through the Capital Transfer Tax which was intended to be more effective than the old Estate Duty. There is also Capital Gains Tax, standing at the comparatively low figure of 30%. An annual Wealth Tax was to be introduced after 1974 but nothing came of this.
2. There is *direct taxation on income* through Income Tax which is a progressive tax since the higher income group pay more.
3. *Indirect taxation* is levied through consumption, VAT and taxes on such things as drink, tobacco and petrol, also through National Insurance contributions and rates. These are all regressive taxes: the same amount is paid by everyone. This means that the rich pay far less (as a percentage of their income) than the poor.

These regressive indirect taxes, which tax the poor proportionally more than the rich, have remarkable consequences. Thus if we arrange householders in receipt of income in ten bands of 10%, we find that in 1974 the top 10% of householders actually paid a lower percentage of their gross salary in taxes than all but one of the nine groups. For example, the top 10% paid 32.7% of their gross income in tax but the bottom 10% paid 33.1% of their gross income in tax. (Report 4, Table 12, RCDIW). This conclusion is borne out by the studies of Professor A. T. Merrett in the USA and J. L. N. Nicholson (*Income and wealth* of Series X edition, Clark and Stuvel), which claim that the British tax system fails to tax the rich more heavily than the poor. It is clear that when the overall tax burden is calculated, the effect of regressive indirect taxes and the low rate of tax on capital gain, together with regressive National Insurance contributions, is to stop any real re-distribution through taxation.

It thus becomes clear that the poor contribute more, pro rata, towards the social benefits they receive than do the rich since the social benefits are financed by taxation, to which the poor contribute a higher proportion of their income. Thus during the period 1964–70 although the lower income groups may be seen as having gained through the expansion of the social services, they paid for this by increased National Insurance contributions which were mainly on the flat rate, that is to say, as a regressive tax which hit the receivers of social benefits harder than the wealthy. What seemed like genuine re-distribution was not re-distribution at all (see *Labour and Inequality*, p. 6f).

POVERTY AND WEALTH IN OUR PRESENT SOCIETY 15

But surely, it will be argued, the poor gained far more than the rich from these social service benefits? Further evidence from the Royal Commission (Report 5, Table 23) discloses an interesting state of affairs. The table compares the effect of taxes and social service benefits on the income of various households. Assuming an average household (2 adults and one to six children) when tax has been deducted and social benefits added to the family income the following changes take place. The richest 10%, who started with 20.7% of the total national income end up having only 18.3% – a loss of 2.4%. By contrast, the poorest 10% start with 3.4% of the total national income. After their tax has been deducted and their benefits added, they end up with 4.5%. This increase of 1.1% suggests that what is being taken from the rich is not actually doing much to help the poor.

The Influence of Wealth

We've already seen that wealth is not merely a matter of cash but also of the quality of life. In addition, it is closely connected with influence. The top 20% in terms of wealth maintain their position because of the influence of their wealth over the rest of the country: its structure, institutions, productivity, and its people's welfare. In the most basic terms, those of ownership, the top 1.25% of the population owns about 70% of all personally held company shares. The top 3.5% (about one million three hundred and seventy thousand people) owns about 90% (see Report 4, Table 25, RCDIW). It may be argued that the percentage of ordinary shares in private ownership has been declining as insurance companies, banks, investment and unit trusts have increased their investment. But personal shareholders still have very strong control through personal shares and unit trusts etc. Pension funds still account for the ownership of only 16% of ordinary shares as compared to 42% in private ownership. There can be no doubt that this small percentage of people controls a major segment of the nation's means of production.

The 3.5% referred to in the previous paragraph holds not only 90% of the personally held company shares but also nearly 96% of the country's privately owned land (see Report 4, Table 25, RCDIW). It thus dominates not only industrial and commercial production but also agricultural production and building. The pattern of ownership of the country's means of production may be more complex now than it was 50 years ago but it is still dominated by a minority.

The Cycle of Inequality

These statistics may be impressive but they give little impression of the truth about poverty. For poverty is not a matter simply of cash but of global deprivation.

Frank Field of the Child Poverty Action Group has identified eight important areas of life between birth and death and researched the levels of inequality existing in each, drawing on all the major research work undertaken since 1945 (*Unequal Britain*, 1974). Basing himself on the customary division of the population into five socio-economic class groups, he shows how people in groups 4 and 5 (semi-skilled and unskilled manual workers) are likely to be caught up in a cycle of inequality which prevents them from breaking out from a life of poverty. This cycle of inequality affects the majority of people in these two groups in every aspect of their lives. Their expectation and achievement differ markedly from those of other groups (professional, non-manual and skilled workers).

Children from the poorer groups start at birth with a lower life expectancy, they are unequal when they start school and this difference grows as their education continues. The same inequality is reflected in adult life through incomes earned, through the status achieved at work and through the accommodation and environmental conditions of the family home. It appears that inequality extends even to the amount of illhealth experienced and to the life expectancy of the different groups. In each of these aspects of life 'class differences in opportunities for life and health start at the cradle and continue through the life-span' (N. D. Bosanquet, 'Inequalities in Health' in *Labour and Inequality*, 1972). The families of semi-skilled and unskilled workers start life with a disadvantage which never leaves them and which they thus transmit ('cycle of inequality') to their children.

So what does it mean in practice to be poor? Among the most influential factors is *housing*. The home and its environment influence both children and parents. The unskilled and semi-skilled in our society exist mainly in the last of the back-to-back terrace housing and the new high-density estates that have replaced them in and around our major cities. The older housing is usually in very bad condition with inadequate facilities. It is often overcrowded with many families living in one house and with bathroom and kitchen facilities being shared. As for the new estates, populating them has meant breaking up the extended family and any sense of community has been lost. Their prison-like tower blocks combine in a concrete jungle. The quality of the new buildings is often low (remember

POVERTY AND WEALTH IN OUR PRESENT SOCIETY

the tower block that fell down in Canning Town?) and this leads to vandalism and disrepair. The density of population is very high (up to 330 people per residential hectare as compared to 70–80 people per hectare in some suburban areas) and this reduces privacy and increases the pressure on the inhabitants. Leisure facilities are often inadequate, there are too few community halls, too little play space for children, little landscaping and no gardens.

What about the *environment*? We have already described conditions on the new estates. As for the older housing – this exists as a twilight area waiting to be pulled down or redeveloped. There are new building sites here and there. There is also a great deal of wasteland full of rubbish tips, many derelict warehouses and dirt and smells and pollution from nearby industrial and factory premises.

And what about the *homeless*? They move continually from one condemned house to another just ahead of the bulldozers or else live in temporary 'half way' houses waiting their turn on the housing list. As the amount of privately rented accommodation has decreased, things have become even worse for these families and particularly for young married couples. For them, as for others in the poorer sectors of society, bad housing means that family life is a source of pain rather than happiness. The environment shapes the lives of their children and moulds them in a way that makes it hard for them to escape.

Education should give young people an equal opportunity in life. But does it? It seems clear that the education system cannot redress the balance of inequality. Thus Ronald Davie, in the National Child Development Study in 1958, found that the chances of the child of a manual worker's family being a non-reader are fifteen times greater than for children from a professional family. Davie also found that there was sometimes as much as four years' difference in reading performance between an advantaged and a disadvantaged child. And even though educational standards have changed much since then, the gap still remains, so we cannot expect education alone to work miracles and redress the balance.

Nor has the comprehensive system come up with any miraculous answer to the problem. Although in principle it is clearly moving in the right direction, various practical points have made it less effective than it could have been. It has suffered because the continued existence of private schools means that we still do not have a comprehensive system. It has not been easy to overcome the difficulties created by having such large schools, particularly in deprived inner city areas. The inadequacy, the pressures, the vandalism and the lack of discipline reflected in the rest of life in those areas becomes extremely difficult to cope with in the confines of a large comprehensive school. The children themselves feel frightened by such large groupings, and fail to gain a sense of friendliness and support needed to cope with life. The fast turnover of staff also makes for instability. Lack of finance also means that the facilities provided are not adequate in terms of space, layout, sports facilities, and landscaping, for the number of pupils involved.

Equal educational opportunity for all is a fine slogan but it has had little effect on the lives of deprived children. Even when they have similar IQs, children from poorer families are less likely to go on to higher and further education as those from richer families. The level of their IQ is of little importance compared with that of the background they come from.

Field's thesis about the cycle of inequality is in accord with the recent White Paper, *Policy for the Inner Cities* (HMSO, 1977). This uses the concept of collective deprivation. Not only do the poor suffer from unequal opportunity in terms of birth, education, income, work, health care and housing – they also suffer from a collective deprivation, when all these are added up, that is greater than the sum of the individual disadvantages.*

'Inner area studies have shown there is a collective deprivation in some areas which affects all the residents, even though individually, the majority of people may have satisfactory homes and worthwhile jobs. It arises from a pervasive sense of decay and neglect which affects the whole area, through the decline of community spirit, through an often low standard of neighbourhood facilities and through greater exposure to crime and vandalism which is a real form of deprivation, above all to old people. All this may make it harder for people to maintain their personal standards and to encourage high standards for their children.... This collective deprivation amounts to more than the sum of all the individual disadvantages with which people have to contend' (para. 17).

To say all this is not to deny that the poor are better off than they used to be. But the gap between poor and rich has scarcely narrowed, let alone closed. Field uses an interesting metaphor. 'The position of the poor has improved. But so too has that of the rich. It is as if the poor have been placed on an escalator which gradually lifts their position. But the rich, too, are on board their own escalator which is moving just as fast, if not faster' (*op. cit.* p. 62). He urges that a new social contract be struck by rich and poor to break the cycle of inequality. The only alternative is a continuation of inequality which in turn could bring conflict to our streets.

* See note on p. 26.

Clearly our society is very deeply divided and unequally structured. However vocal our superficial concern to 'do good' or to 'help people in need' there has not been a realistic move to equality. The forces that maintain the present structure of society seem stronger than the desire for equal opportunity. The ratio between rich and poor, between wealth and poverty, between surplus and deprivation has remained constant or even deteriorated. But before asking why the widespread concern to reduce inequality has been so ineffective, we may note another way in which an attempt has been made to alleviate poverty and, to a certain extent, to reduce inequality.

Is Community Development the Answer?

The traditional methods of combating inequality have been taxation and expanding the social services. More recently, a third approach has been adopted. Study surveys have focused on the intense deprivation of inner city areas with a view to recommending specific changes to improve the situation. By injecting finance into the economy of the inner cities, successive governments have hoped to re-vitalise them and hence to bring greater prosperity.

These modern urban programmes began in U.S.A. in the 1960's. Starting in President Kennedy's time, they led on to President Johnson's Poverty Programme 1964–66 and to the Model Cities Programme 1966–70. The thinking behind these programmes is well analysed in *The Dilemma of Social Reform* (Morris & M. Rein). The desire for an urban programme to ease the deprivation of the inner cities emerged in Britain in 1968 under the special Urban Aid Programme. Studies included the Plowden, Seebolm and Skeffington Reports on Education, Social Services and Planning, in general; then in particular the Educational Priority Areas (1968–70) the Shelter Neighbourhood Action project (1969–72), Community Development projects (1970–77) the Inner Area studies (1973–76), the Area Management Trials (1976) and the Comprehensive Community programme (1976), Sir Keith Joseph's Cycle of Deprivation studies, and Peter Walker's 'Six Town Studies' culminating in the Government White Paper *Policy for the Inner Cities* in June 1977.

These surveys have resulted in various analyses and recommendations, some of which have been supported by government money. Several reasons have been given for the concentration of poverty and inequality within an area. Firstly, it has been suggested that the residents are trapped in a *cycle of deprivation* through inadequacy or deviancy. Secondly, it has been suggested that the low take-up of available services or even the offering of inappropriate services, is a result of the *technical incompetence of local government*, seen in insufficient planning, co-ordination, communication and consultation between the local authority and the public. Thirdly, the communities have been found to be *apathetic about community activity and self-help schemes*. The surveys have suggested that if all of these points were remedied, with a certain amount of financial assistance, the scene would change. Thus, given a determination to eliminate these areas of poverty, it should be possible to provide positive discrimination in favour of the deprived and thus lift the living standards of the poorest.

Some people, however, have criticised both the analysis and the remedies suggested. Marxists in particular have argued that the roots of social distress and inequality go far deeper.

(See the final reports of the Community Development Projects and research at the University of Birmingham (1977) on the Inner Area Studies (1973–76) Reports.)

The argument advanced is that such urban distress throws up the basic conflict underlying the present distribution of power; it is political and economic forces that are the major instruments in maintaining the high level of deprivation. The underlying causes are said to be economic. Far from being an unfortunate by-product of a mainly successful advanced urban system, the poverty and deprivation of the inner city is an intrinsic part of the capitalist system, and cannot be eradicated by superficial changes. A radical reappraisal of the political and economic balance is necessary since any real long-term change will result only from fundamental shifts in power and resources.

How the System Resists Change

The government White Paper, *Policy for the Inner Cities*, 1977, recognises at one point that its urban programmes can never totally succeed because of certain social processes over which the programme has little control. The root cause of inequality seems to lie far more in the structure of our society than in the personal character and ability of individuals or in changing physical and social conditions. If it is essential to the capitalist system that the inequality ratio between rich and poor should remain stable, then the only way to reduce inequality is by questioning and re-structuring the economic order. So far, we have sought to reduce inequality and poverty through ways that do not affect what Lord Balfour called the 'foundation of our society', the existing economic and social system of private ownership and appropriation.

In order to do this, we must identify where the greatest concentration of power lies within our society since it is such power that determines whether poverty is allowed to continue or whether it is reduced. This is no easy task since power is not a tangible phenomenon and although its effects can be identified its precise location is more difficult to find.

It is often assumed that the real source of power in our society lies in the hands of people. As we shall see later, although our society is theoretically a democratic one, massive powers are in practice exercised by a minute percentage of the population. However, the power of control over our society is not limited to individuals or groups of people. As John Westergaard has pointed out (*Class in a Capitalist Society*, Westergaard and Resler, pp. 141ff) power is also achieved by anonymous social mechanisms, assumptions and principles. Power can be obtained and enjoyed purely by taking advantage of 'the way things are'. 'In a Capitalist society the social mechanisms and assumptions which are generally taken for granted in this way are those, in the first instance, of private property and the market. It is they which largely determine the living conditions of the people and the use of resources. And they clearly favour the interest of capital.... It is taken for granted that "in the way things work" that profit should be the normal yardstick of investment in most areas of activity, that the living standards of the propertyless majority should be set primarily by the terms on which they sell or once sold their labour' (*ibid.*, p. 143). So power to control within our society, the forces that directly affect the incidence of poverty and its persistence depends not so much on direct action or decision by a small group of powerful individuals, but rather on the routine and unquestioned application of social mechanisms and principles, that benefit those with capital and property and deprive the poor.

How have the Structures Changed?

In spite of the shift in power and the continuing ideological debate between unions and employers, some basic questions are still not being asked. By predetermining the bounds of discussion and conflict, those who now hold power are able to perpetuate accepted social principles and assumptions and thus maintain their position. Quite often it is suggested that extreme capitalist domination is a thing of the past. Various reasons are adduced in support of this statement. Managerial power has eroded the power of ownership. State involvement has reduced the private sector. We are now a pluralist economy. Yet, as we have seen, the inequality remains. Wealth, land and industrial control still remain in the hands of a select group which continues to perpetuate itself.

In one respect indeed, it could be argued that the size of the power-exercising minority is being reduced whilst its influence is growing. The rise and growth of multinational companies has certainly had this effect. In 1969 the hundred largest manufacturing firms in the United Kingdom accounted for only 16% of the total net output in the manufacturing industry. By 1970 the hundred largest firms were responsible for 41% of the total output and 47% of the capital expenditure in the industry. In 1967 the sales turnover of Ford was larger than the total Gross National Product of such European countries as Belgium, Norway and Switzerland and Denmark (cf. *Invisible Empires – Multinational Companies and the Modern World* – L. Turner, pp. 135–6).

There are other, more subtle ways, in which a minority achieves power in this country. People sometimes suggest that class dominance is a thing of the past but it is still with us. A classic paper by T. Lupton and C. S. Wilson (*Power in Britain*, Chapter 14) shows to what a remarkable extent the leaders in our society are linked through education, wealth, social clubs and family ties. Although there is no official 'closed shop' many key positions are, as a rule, open only to those who are accepted by a particular social group. Such key positions would be those of cabinet ministers and members of Parliament, senior personnel of the armed services and civil services, ambassadors, diplomats and chairmen of government committees of inquiry and royal commissions, governors and directors of Bank of England and the 'big five' banks and directors of major city firms, insurance companies and commercial companies, the judiciary, the B.B.C., the universities and even the House of Bishops.

In their study Lupton and Wilson divided these positions of power into six groups and analysed some of the social attributes of those holding them. They found that a high proportion was educated at one of the top six public schools. (About 50% of all government ministers, directors of the Bank of England, directors of the 'big five' banks and of the major insurance companies.) They also found that about 70% of government ministers and top civil servants, 50% of bank directors and just under 40% of the directors of city firms and insurance companies had also graduated from either Oxford or Cambridge. A survey of social clubs and family connections yielded similar results. It is clear that 'top people' are a close knit group not only in virtue of the positions they hold but also because they have known and grown up with each other through school, university, social pursuits and inter-marriage. Many are following relations who occupied the same positions of power before them.

Such a group will certainly draw in new owners of wealth and managers of wealth. But although it is not static, it will still maintain its own ethos and exclusiveness and the same determination to hold on to power and wealth, however much it may appear to have changed.

This small socio-economic group is in a position to dominate politics, the civil service, the city and business, the judiciary and the armed forces. Inevitably, it influences what the state does or does not do, not only as regards poverty and inequality but in every sphere. The men in the City of London have only to say to the men in Whitehall that a given policy would lead to a 'loss of confidence in the pound' for that policy to be rescinded. As long ago as 1902, Kara Kautskes pointed out that 'the capitalist class rules but does not govern, it contents itself with ruling the government' (*The Social Revolution*, p. 13). This frightening concentration of power can in effect tie the hands of the state if it were to attempt anything that might damage the economic position of the top decision-makers. And it is these people who, collectively and individually, have the last word in deciding whether or not to implement policies leading to real reductions in inequality.

A Dilemma

In examining this question of inequality and poverty within our society we have uncovered a challenging moral dilemma. There is an increasing concern to provide equality of opportunity and to reduce the poverty that some people experience but when this demand is made then the system of private ownership and private property finds itself on trial. The demand for equality reveals a central conflict between the desire for economic efficiency, essential for the capitalist enterprise, and the desire for distributive justice, essential for any society that has chosen to offer future generations equality of opportunity.

It is not surprising that many people now argue that real equality can't come until the present system is radically changed. They point out that in view of the massive imbalance of power we have indicated, it is pointless to try 'tinkering with the system'. Those who argue in this way are not impressed by claims that parity exists today between capital/business and labour/trades unions so that equality should ultimately come about as the result of the inter-action of these two major interests. For as Ralph Miliband has shown (*Power in Britain*, Chapter 10), in reality the influence of capital is far stronger than that of labour. It is better organised, less divided, it has unity of purpose in maintaining the present system, it has far closer connections with Government and administration and it has the overall power of wealth to back it. It has close links with the international finance interests which are also totally committed to the same inequality so created. So attempts to tinker with the situation seem doomed to failure.

Such an attitude will necessarily affect our attitude to conflict within society. If at the heart of society there is such a clash between the various interest groups and if in that clash inequality is made worse as the 'status quo' wins again and again, it may arguably be a good thing for these conflicts of interest to come to a head. Perhaps the radical re-structuring thus made necessary would bring a fairer distribution of wealth and equality. Society might then re-consider its values. Instead of the norms and value of the wealthy elite being accepted as binding on the whole of society, other interest groups in society might be allowed to take part in the formation of new norms reflecting a far greater cross-section of thought and attitudes than at present (see *Social Values, Social Class, Social Policy* by V. P. Wilding – Social Administration Conference, Nottingham, 1972). It thus becomes possible to see conflict in positive terms as the only way to achieve a greater degree of equality in our society. Certainly tinkering with the system, although it has considerable practical advantages for those who benefit from the system, appears more and more inadequate to deal with the root causes of inequality.

What is the alternative? We have seen that the persistence of poverty within our society is a fact to be reckoned with. We have seen that it is possible to decline to define the reasons for its persistence. Those who ultimately control our society accept this inequality. They see it as a factor of minor importance in human life, although an abnormality which should be controlled and reduced if at all possible. They propose doing so by adapting certain aspects of the present system and making some money available for 'ambulance work in the guise of social benefits for the poor'. They see nothing unjust in the present distribution of wealth and income and therefore no reason to change it. They depend on the economical efficiency of the present system for their own wealth and are unwilling to sacrifice this in the interests of greater distributive justice in wealth and power. What is frightening and amazing is that this attitude towards inequality is being increasingly accepted in a society that claims to be growing more egalitarian. 'When incontrovertible evidence of persistent and substantial inequality has been with us for some considerable time, there is perhaps today a greater degree of reconciliation to prevailing conditions of social inequality than for many years' (*Power in Britain*, J. Wakeford, p. 322).

An International Issue

This issue is not only a national one but an international one. Just as the wealthy minority in Britain protects its interests against the poor majority, so the industrial West maintains its position over against the countries of the developing Third World. Although it is often imagined that as Third World countries become more developed they reduce the wealth gap between themselves and the Industrial West, this is not so. International statistics on wealth follow the same pattern as the 'lessening of inequality' national figures. Indeed it is argued that the richer countries are actually growing even richer still in comparison to the Third World. The national statistics show a frightening gap between rich and poor; so do the international ones: as many as 2,000 million people live in countries where the gross national product is around £100 per head and as few as 600 million live in countries with a gross national product of between £1,000 and £3,000 per head (see *Towards a New International Economic Order* – Commonwealth Secretariat, 1977).

According to a recent United Nations study, entitled *The Future of the World Economy*, this gap, which was estimated in 1970 as being in the ratio of 12:1, is not expected even to begin closing before the year 2,000. Just as the persistence of inequality is a real challenge to our own society, so is it in the international order. Nationally and internationally, the impression given is that inequality is being reduced. Yet in reality nothing of the sort is happening.

In view of all that has been said in this chapter, it is important for Christians to know what is the church's position. What is its past and present record? What is the church's attitude to inequality, deprivation and poverty? What is it doing about oppression? What is the church's relationship with the wealthy and the élite, the powerful and the decision-makers? And how does the church relate to the poor, the working-class and the oppressed?

In this book we shall study the views of the church on inequality and its persistence but we shall go further and examine also some of the views of the biblical writers in order to discover whether the church is or is not being true to the biblical witness.

At this point it may be as well to define what is meant in this book by the word 'church'. Basically, the book is about the views and attitudes of what we may call the 'English Church'. Before the Reformation, the church was the church *in* England, loyal also to Rome. After the Reformation, the church became the 'Church of England' with less and less European influence. Later the church in England was not only the Church of England but also included non-conformist churches. The 'church' is the sum total of all these churches as they express the Christian faith. Some of the material in this book may reflect more on the Church of England than on the non-conformist churches. But whatever differences may be seen from the inside, the churches' approach to external questions of inequality, wealth and poverty has tended to be uniform although where differences have occurred, they will be noted.

Note

Further examples of extreme deprivation have been strongly claimed by members of ethnic groups such as West Indian and Asian communities. A clear illustration of such claims is given by Gus John in the B.C.C. publication *The New Black Presence in Britain*. Seeing themselves discriminated against in education, housing, employment, they also feel blamed unjustly for causing ghetto areas, and racial hatred in communities where the potentiality and/or actuality of both were already present.

CHAPTER TWO

The Church, the Status Quo and Inequality in the Present Day

Having recognised the existence of extremes of poverty and wealth in our society, and the inadequacy of the attempts to reduce such extremes, we now investigate the church's response to the situation today. We need to see how the church reacts to the poverty and inequality that exists all around it. We need to recognise its failure to appreciate poverty and inequality, and its avoidance of the issue when it does see it. We need to recognise its failure to separate itself sufficiently from society, the state and their unwritten assumptions and moral values in order to be able to criticise effectively what is happening. In general, the church seems oblivious to the fact that the present economic and social system is contributing to the maintenance of poverty and inequality, and that this same system is silently annexing and enslaving the church. The church seems equally unaware of how much it is serving and supporting the wealthy rather than the poor, and how its vested interests and its social connections are separating it from the example and commands of Jesus to serve the poor.

1. Uncritical Acceptance of Key Principles within Society's View of Poverty and Inequality

a) *Inadequate explanations of the persistence of poverty and inequality*

Some common explanations of poverty and inequality have been uncritically endorsed by Christians without serious thought. One theory is that poverty and the persistence of poverty has *biological roots*, being caused neither by oppression nor by injustice but rather by biological and hereditary factors. As in the animal kingdom some are born weak and others strong, so weakness and poverty may be hereditary. The consequent cycle of poverty or deprivation makes it impossible for the individual or the family to escape.

Poverty can therefore be seen as an integral part of the human landscape. Life is a matter of the 'survival of the fittest' and therefore an element of poverty amongst the weakest is inescapable and also acceptable. If the causes are biological, economic or political factors in society cannot significantly change the situation. 'The poor will always be with us' it is said. Some might even suggest that in order to eliminate poverty we should encourage breeding by the strongest and discourage it in the weakest. Other claim that inequality in fact reduces poverty, since the strongest, as they develop, are bound to raise the living standards of the weakest at the same time – the 'trickle down' theory. It is therefore argued that the best way to reduce such biologically induced poverty is to increase the incentives society offers the strongest so that they actually raise the overall standard of living and hence alleviate the conditions of those trapped in the cycle of poverty.

This biological view makes it possible to blame Nature (or the Creator) for poverty. Poverty is programmed into the creation and there is little man can do about it. Many Christians would subscribe to such a viewpoint even though it raises intensely difficult theological questions. These Christians do not take seriously the belief that God made every man in his image, and that he made all men equal, nor do they take into account the fall of man: the greed of one person that produces poverty for another. They do not appreciate that human poverty is evil in God's eyes, and therefore to be eliminated because it is antipathetic to the Kingdom of God. They fail to grasp that God, working through his people could actually eliminate poverty, if only his followers realised the possibility.

Some see *the social environment* as equally significant, pointing out that some people will automatically become poor because they fail to respond to their environment. Society is essentially competitive, and any successful system must allow free enterprise to hold sway, allowing those who are strong to get even stronger. They will then pressurise the weak but it is claimed that this cannot be helped, due to inborn inequality. Anyway the poor will be helped because of the 'trickle-down' effect mentioned above.

Many Christians are committed to this view, thinking that free enterprise is the only viable system and that it makes by far the most

THE CHURCH, THE STATUS QUO AND INEQUALITY

of the human potential available. They do not consider that the whole free enterprise system might be a major cause of such poverty, or that poverty could be alleviated by changing that system or that there must be equality of opportunity for everyone at the start, which is demonstrably not so at present.

A third view is that of the determinist who claims that 'what will be – will be': the cycle of poverty however it started, is with us and cannot now be stopped, because it is too deeply engrained, and our bureaucratic system is too unwieldy to reprogramme. There is insufficient will-power amongst those who are successful and who actually control the system to change it in favour of someone else, and the changes required would be so central to the system itself that logistically it would be impossible, and technologically it would be regressive.

It is quite true that in human terms our future seems strongly determined by our present and past. But such fatalism surely contracts the whole vision of the Christian faith. Christ said 'I have come to make all things new'. Christians should be looking for the signs of the New Kingdom where things are going to be very different. Christians should not believe that the world's estate is totally determined for they believe in the power of the Holy Spirit to change the present world into a new Kingdom, that has already started and will one day be fully realised – a Kingdom where poverty can have no place. The dynamic of Jesus Christ is the exact opposite to the dynamic of determinism.

b) *Complacent Acceptance of the Capitalist Spiral*

The Church accepts the way society works in Britain – the democratic system of Government, the capitalist system of the economy, and the judicial system that enforces both. It assumes that this system is working, however slowly, towards a reduction in inequality, poverty and suffering, and that it is succeeding. It considers that such a structure is working for the greatest good of the greatest number. And as no viable alternative has been presented, the church supports and backs up the present system.

But the church is being deceived into thinking that it is supporting a structure that is concerned with the ideals and principles that the Christian faith stands for; an end to poverty and a reduction in inequality. For however much society would like to think that it stands for such ideals, there is little evidence of any such achievement.

One of the main virtues claimed for a capitalist structure such as ours is that it gives *everyone* greater wealth and thereby reduces poverty and inequality. Free enterprise and the investment of private capital means that those who invest make a profit and at the same time provide employment, and hence income for others who do not have capital, but only their own labour to use. The more the wealthy are able to profit, the more will be available all the way through to the workforce; and even through the social services via taxation to the unemployed and pensioners. This is the theory of 'trickle down' which argues that everyone benefits from an economically efficient free enterprise system. So as long as those with wealth, hold on to it and use it, they will enable many others to escape from inequality and poverty. However, this system does not actually work in the way suggested: for it makes no change at all in the ratio between rich and poor. The poor indeed get richer, but so do the rich. So the gap between the two stays the same and inequality in society remains. Because the whole standard of living goes up, all the increased wealth the poor receive hardly enables them to keep abreast of increases in price. As long as wages go up only at the same percentage as price increases and divided payments, the real increase in the poor person's income will be only marginal at best. The claim that the success of the rich brings with it a reduction in inequality and poverty cannot be substantiated. The assumption that what is good for the rich is good also for the poor is misleading and can easily add to the confusion about poverty rather than help to alleviate it.

Another claim made by advocates of the present system is that as economic efficiency is maintained by private enterprise and as growth of output is achieved, then there is more surplus money available to help directly those who are caught in the poverty trap. Such economic success means that social benefits can be expanded, and considerable finance poured into urban areas to eliminate the deprivation there. So economic gain is taxed and thus used to finance social benefits and urban aid. But as we have already seen, this still makes little real difference to the inequality ratio.

Another objection to this approach is that, while the poor may benefit financially, they may also be made more 'dependent' and hence 'poor', since they *receive* assistance, which is achieved by someone else rather than by themselves. Active assistance on the other hand would *encourage* those who are deprived to work for themselves provided that changes were made to enable them to achieve real parity with others. 'Active' support for the poor would mean not only encouraging them to work their way out of poverty, but would also involve a commitment to restructure society, so that inequality would be reduced, fairer distribution achieved, and equal opportunity made available to all.

THE CHURCH, THE STATUS QUO AND INEQUALITY 31

2. Complacent Acceptance of Key Capitalist Principles

If the church has been deceived by the claims of the state to be beneficent, it has also been beguiled into accepting the principles inherent in the state system, which remains more capitalist than Christian.

a) *Profit*

Poverty and hence inequality is actually essential for the continuation of capitalism. For instance capital is normally invested in areas of the greatest profit. Harvey (*Social Justice and the City*, p. 112) has pointed out that in geographical terms, this means that capital can rarely be induced into areas of deprivation where the return is low; deprived areas will therefore continue as such, because they cannot attract private capital for their development.* If capital goes to the point of greatest profit then other areas of society will necessarily remain deprived. The deprivation of the inner cities becomes therefore an intrinsic part of the system (and there is little that the recent Government initiatives can do about it).

The general policy trends of the big multinational companies (and these have an increasingly tight grip on the whole of the British manufacturing industry) have been increasingly to place their re-investment programme in areas of the highest profit yield. This has meant that new investment has often been placed in other countries, where labour costs are lower, rather than in English cities where it is desperately needed. So areas in the inner cities that are already suffering, are forced to suffer more because it is not in the interests of industrial finance to invest where there is a low profit return even though there is a high degree of human need there (cf. *Unemployment and the Multinationals in Coventry* – Coventry Workshop, 1978). In addition cutting costs has meant installing more automated plant, doing little to alleviate high unemployment.

If the level of profit is the yardstick for investment and capital outlay, then people will often suffer because their needs conflict with the need for the greatest profit. Inequality will always remain because, the need for the highest profit from investment will normally be stronger than personal needs. This is because an intrinsic principle of the system is that 'Profits even though not the ultimate goal, are the necessary means to all ultimate goals. As such they become the immediate unique, unifying, quantitative aim

---

* Harvey recognises that Government incentive schemes can be a means of redressing such inbalance, but he suggests that often such incentives do not work in the long term because the more attractive investment areas then offer greater incentives that tend to draw the investment back to them again (cf. *ibid.*, p. 113).

of corporate policies, the touchstone of corporate rationality, the measure of corporate success' (Baran and Sweeny – *Monopoly Capital*, p. 40). The price of profit for one man may often be a loss of humanity for another man, whether in direct terms such as conditions of work in a factory, or in indirect terms such as the low level of private investment in a deprived inner city area which leads to bad housing, environment, and employment opportunities for those who live there.

b) *Balance of Power*

Another principle condoned by the church, and lying at the heart of the present system, concerns the relationship between capital and labour. Most economic production depends on an alliance of two major interests; the investment of capital, and the availability of labour. Capital and labour join forces at the point of production to produce a commodity that is then sold. Clearly then, the relationship between the two in the initial contract is all important. If there is an imbalance of power or sharing at that point, the development of inequality will follow. To have a contract that is fair and equal to both sides is essential, and it should be entered into freely by both parties. Although this is the ideal, it doesn't often happen. Under the influence of the existing system, and with the capital/labour relations that have developed ever since the Industrial Revolution, contracts today are often not balanced fairly, and are often not entered into freely by both sides. Because of this inequality arises at the very point of production.

Workers enter the contract with a commodity: they have their labour to sell. Employers and investors enter with their commodity: capital to invest and management expertise. In theory it ought to be possible to balance out the advantage, but in practice this doesn't happen. For the worker when he sells his labour then has no more to dispose of, whereas the investor and the management have not invested all that they have. This means that one party has far greater control over the ensuing processes. Hence capital rather than labour dominates much of the decision making from then on. Such decisions are concerned with what to produce, at what price to sell it, where to look for markets, what level reinvestment should reach, the nature of work conditions, levels of automation, and redundancy and what ratio there should be between wage rises and dividend payments. The 'Capital' side alone has all the facts and figures about the enterprise and so becomes the only party qualified to make major policy decisions. Labour still retains some power through the use of strike action, but this is very variable and depends on the particular commodity concerned. That power is also reduced when it threatens the overall national economic enterprise. Present-day governments have been able to reduce the power of labour still further through incomes policies which lessen opportunities to strike.

It is not only at the point of production that this imbalance of power between capital and labour expresses itself. There is also an imbalance at a general or national level. It has been argued that our pluralist society allows all sectors to bring pressure to bear so that their needs can be heard and met. But Ralph Miliband (*The State and Capitalist Society, and Power in Britain*, Chapter 10) has suggested very strongly that this does not actually work out in practice. Although it is thought that the two major veto groups (capital and labour) balance each other out, he argues that this does not happen because the power behind the two is not equal and so no equilibrium exists. He suggests that capital exerts far more pressure on the economy, on the government, and on the structure of society, because it has far more wide-ranging power. Its owners are better organised, more single-minded, and appear to have 'the good of the country' as their purpose. It is also bound up with major industrial and international financial interests. Labour is far more fragmented and divided. The Trades Unions lack both the same wealth and power base, because there are no such strong links with the powerful and wealthy decision-makers. So at national level and at the point of production, the unequal relationship between capital and labour, results in the continuation, and often extension, of inequality in our society. Inequality does not just happen; it is a direct result of principles that, once established, perpetuate and reinforce it.

c) *Ownership – Stewardship*

The third of these principles which the church accepts is ownership. This has a very real connection with poverty and inequality; indeed it could be claimed that it is one of the root causes of the persistence of inequality. There are two reasons for this: the first relates to the nature of ownership, and the second to how it is achieved. The first point, will be fully dealt with in the next chapter, but can be mentioned here.

The view taken by society is that ownership is an inalienable right. If someone owns something, it is his by right and he can do what he wants with it, and also with whatever it produces. The owner has the right both to outright ownership, and also to the use of everything produced from what he owns. This view, although a seemingly fair and just one, is not totally compatible with the biblical view. Where society claims that ownership is the right of man, the Bible claims that it is the right of God. Man is seen more as a steward than an owner. He is expected to look after property, but the right to consume all that is produced from it is not necessarily his. This difference of approach to the meaning of ownership has a real bearing on the persistence of equality. For if the secular view is taken, inequality and poverty are encouraged; if the biblical view is taken they are discouraged. The church's unquestioning tolerance of the former view is another example of its failure to realise that (often unconsciously) it is encouraging, rather than discouraging, the growth of inequality all around it.

How has ownership been achieved? There is, as any simple study of history will show, ample evidence that our present distribution of wealth and ownership has been achieved by highly doubtful methods. By Christian standards ownership has regularly been achieved at the expense of other people's basic human rights. Members of the ruling class used their power over others to control all means of production in society so that they were able to take a vast percentage of the profits for themselves; passing on only a very small amount to the work force whose labour made the whole enterprise possible. The accumulation of this wealth subsequently left that sector in a stronger bargaining position. Therefore in the situations brought about by the industrial or agricultural revolutions, those who were in a position of power, were able to pressurise the weaker members of society into a work contract that was highly detrimental to them; a contract that shared out the profits of the enterprise unequally.

Certainly the distribution of wealth would be very different today if everyone's basic equality had been taken into account in the past. Obviously within present distribution some of the extreme wealth that exists today has been accumulated by careful saving on the part of the owner rather than through exploitation, but that cannot dispel completely the real element of truth that lies behind Miranda's words when he says 'Not one ounce of the capital which exists today could have been generated if the workers of our countries had been able to exercise their natural and inalienable right to organise as workers and consumers' (*Marx and the Bible*, p. 11).

The evidence of this pattern has been with us for a long time. St. Chrysostom writes on the subject: 'Tell me how it is that you are rich? ... From where did you receive your wealth? ... From the grandfather you say, from the father. By climbing the genealogical tree, are you able to show the justice of this possession? Of course not, you cannot – rather its beginnings and root have necessarily come out of injustice.' And St. Jerome writes: 'Unless one person has lost another cannot find. Therefore I believe that the popular proverb is true "The rich person is either an unjust person or the heir to one"'.

We could see also injustices in wealth gained by many very powerful families and businesses through the slave trade. This wealth has never been returned even though the descendants of the traders might abhor the idea of slavery today. Other examples can be found in England's use of its colonies and empire, in the past. There is no doubt that the amount of wealth, expertise, and education, given to the colonies by England was minuscule, when compared with the value of the raw materials and products that she obtained at ridiculously low prices from the colonies for her own growth and wealth. The same situation obtains, even today, between Britain and the Third World.

There is plenty of evidence that exploitation is still with us. J. Miranda writes in *Marx and the Bible* (p. 11): 'When the Marshall Plan for war-torn West Germany was begun, Nell-Breuning posed this problem: who will repay these American loans? Obviously the consumers, for by means of prices the business will collect the money necessary to repay the Americans. But at the end of the reconstruction who will be the owners of the factories and all the machinery of production? Obviously the Krupps and the Thyssens and the capitalist class in general. The means of the production will be paid for by the workers who labour and consume; but they will be the private property of a handful of families. And so there occurred the German miracle, as it was called, and indeed in fifteen or twenty years the industries, the commercial chains, the automobile and truck fleets, the banks, etc, etc, were reconstructed stronger than ever. The workers paid for all this by enduring high prices for goods and services that could have cost them much less. The workers paid for all of it and none of it belongs to them. Private ownership is robbery, legalised, institutionalised, civilised, canonised robbery.'

And so the evidence mounts up that the present distribution of wealth and power is unfair and unjust and that the church turns a blind eye to it.

3. Complacent Acceptance of Certain Moral Values

There are also moral questions on which the church has failed to take a Christian stand but instead has tamely accepted the norms of society. By accepting society's views on such matters, the church is, indirectly, contributing towards the growth of inequality, and detracting from the dignity of man.

a) *Man as a Producer*

Since the Industrial Revolution, man has become a servant of the production of goods. He can no longer be described as an individual created by God to have dominion over the whole of the created order. Man, it seems, is now dominated by the material order that he should be dominating; in both industry and leisure, he takes second place to the product he is producing. Production therefore is seen no longer as a means whereby man can enrich and fulfil his whole personality, but solely as a way of producing material assets, that can in turn be consumed. Consumption of goods has become over-important, and has displaced man, and all his needs, in the process. All those other qualities, that should be developed in order to encourage equality and justice for all, have been at the least degraded, and sometimes completely lost. 'When it (capital economy) must choose between capital and man, it will always choose capital' (Archb. Helder Camara – *Structures of Injustice, Justice and Peace Commission*, 1972, p. 5). What is now being worshipped is no longer the humanity of man, but rather the production of materials to be consumed, and the maximum profit obtainable in the process. The quality of a man's life may be forgotten. Equality and justice become secondary to the overall necessity for profit, and are not allowed to interfere with the process of production.

b) *Economics*

Society's moral values must again be questioned with regard to economics. For in this realm, as in production, man is reduced to the level of serving economic necessity. In other words, if an issue arises, it can be accepted or rejected on purely economic grounds. Other values are hardly taken into consideration. The value put on man's life is therefore reduced to a quantitive level alone and the qualitative values in life, are given only secondary importance. Unless an enterprise brings profit to its owner it will not be judged economically viable and without this viability it will not be considered even if it carries many other benefits. Piere Bigo describes this as the 'debasement of man by the primacy which the economic world has gained over him' (*Marxismo y humanismo*, p. 234). Values such as equality, justice, beauty, honesty, virtue, trust and sincerity, have become secondary to the primary values of economics. The pollution of the environment, and the exhausting of the world's resources, are not considered obnoxious in themselves; they are seen as bad, only because, if they continue, they will jeopardise man's economic position. Man has reduced his stature from that of a steward to that of a mere consumer.

c) *Pragmatism*

In politics too, at a local and international level, decisions are made according to economic or practical factors, rather than moral ones. Solzhenitsyn has highlighted this attitude in his devastating criticisms of the West. He has claimed that the West's response to Russian aggression in Africa, Indo-China and the Middle East is based far more on pragmatic than moral grounds. His criticism has been confirmed in the attitude of England towards South Africa, where although there is moral disagreement with the policy of 'apartheid', no action will ever be taken that might be detrimental to Britain's massive financial investments in that country. On such issues as these, moral principles are placed below economic and pragmatic reasons.

d) *Status*

This is perhaps the most subtle way in which society devalues man. People who work in certain professions – medicine, social work, the police, etc, have limited earnings and long working hours and, except locally, their work may go un-noticed. Popstars, sportsmen, film stars and media pundits on the other hand can earn vast sums and are always in the public eye. More importance is attached to news-worthiness than to the good of society, and society suffers morally from this perverted attitude. The church has allowed these inequalities and injustices to persist within the heart of society, apparently unconcerned by what is happening all around her. It would appear that she is even prepared to go along with Lord Keynes' recommendation: 'For another hundred years we must pretend to ourselves and to everyone that fair is foul and foul is fair; for foul is useful and fair is not. Avarice and usury and precaution must be our gods for a little longer still.'

4. The Church's Continued Allegiance to the Wealthy and Powerful

It is often difficult, particularly from within, to appreciate the extent and nature of this relationship between the wealthy and the church. It is easy to explain away the situation, but an objective assessment reveals far more of the true nature of the relationship. Such helpful objectivity has often come from Christians in Third World countries who have looked at the church in the West and analysed perceptively the strength of its relationship to those in power. They have brought to light the way in which the church accepts unquestioningly Western capitalist values. They can also see in practice how Western Christians lean far more towards wealth than towards poverty.

This analysis is put most penetratingly in a paper given by S. Escobar to the 1974 World Conference on Evangelism in Lausanne. He makes a point that pierces to the very heart of the attitudes taken by the Western Church, (the English Church included) today: that the church who is called to be the 'servant' of all men, is in reality, still in the position of 'master'. The position of the Church today does not match up to its message and has not done so since the time of Constantine. Pursuing his image of the world as a village of 100 people of which only 7 are North Americans, Escobar pointed out: 'As part of the wealthy 7, we (the Church) are trying to reach as many of the other 93 for Christ as we can; we tell them about Jesus and they watch us throw away more food than they can ever hope to eat. We are busy building beautiful church buildings and they scramble to find shelter for their families. We have money in the bank, and they do not have enough to buy food for their children. All the while we tell them that our Master was the servant of men, the Saviour who gave his all for us and bids us give our all for him.... We are the rich minority of the world. We may be able to forget about that, or consider it unimportant. The question is, can the 93 forget?' Escobar's example, while taken from a North American standpoint, also relates just as directly to the English church's attitude to the Third World. It shows clearly how, as part of the wealthy élite of mankind, we are unconcerned about the needs of the poor; a devasting criticism of any so called follower of Christ. It just as clearly describes the attitude of the church towards the poor and underprivileged in England today, for the church is still identified with the wealthy in society, and is still out of touch with a vast percentage of the British population today, who are poor rather than rich.

The church is still held in the strait jacket that it has made for itself over the past 1,000 years, by its commitment to the wealthy élite and their philosophy. It cannot extricate itself without a revolution based on biblical principles. Having accepted the norms of society uncritically, it is now being emasculated by them. The vested interests that have served and strengthened the church's powerful and wealthy position in the past, now will not let her go, and the establishment that she has built up needs massive wealth to make it work:

so she cannot afford to break with her influential friends. Those in power who have always benefited from having the church's blessing on all their activities, certainly don't want a revolution at a time when the capitalist principle is being questioned.

Let us now consider some examples of the liaison between the church and the wealthy, in both practical and intellectual spheres of life. To do so, we shall consider one denomination more than the others, because statistics are more readily available. The relationship however applies to other denominations though with various differences.

The Church of England reflects the whole church *in* England in that it has a bias towards the wealthy rather than the poor. It continues to be the church of the privileged members of society rather than the deprived, being strongest amongst those who benefit from inequality, and weakest amongst those who suffer from it. In geographical terms, its strongest support comes from the suburban and rural commuter areas, and its weakest links are in the inner cities, the large council housing estate areas, and among the rural poor. Such a bias starts from the very top and works its way down through each level of the church.

At the top, it is dominated by two groups, the bishops and the General Synod, both of which have distinct affiliations. The bishops have always had strong connections with the upper and upper middle classes, especially through their education. Morgan's work (*Social and Educational Background of English Diocesan Bishops in the Church of England 1860–1960*) has brought this clearly to light. And although these influences are less than in the previous century, they are nevertheless still there. In 1860 all diocesan bishops were connected either by birth or by marriage to the peerage or the 'landed' upper classes. In 1960, one would have expected the link to be more tenuous, but even then over half the bishops had similar links and there were no diocesan bishops with working class connections. In 1958 Harvey and Hood's survey showed that 66% went to Public Schools, and they all had University education (88% going to Oxford or Cambridge). In 1975 those figures were only slightly lower. Out of all the bishops in the General Synod, over 60% had a Public School education, there were only two non-graduates, 80% of the graduates coming from Oxford or Cambridge (cf. *Analysis of General Synod*. Prof. Kathleen Jones of York University. Crucible Oct.–Dec. 1976). Clearly as a leadership group the bishops are distinct in both their social backgrounds and their education. They all come from social class 1 (in the Registrar General's five point scale) often by birth and certainly through education. Their experience is of such an élitist world that their decisions will almost inevitably reflect this background.

The other dominant group in the leadership of the church is the General Synod; it is the parliament of the church, and is supposed to be a democratic decision-making body. Such a body obviously influences the life of the church very strongly, and so its social connections are very important, and quite revealing. It is made up of three houses, the first of which (the House of Bishops) we have already considered. The second house is confined to clergy. Once again, they all tend to come from social class 1 or 2 (on the R.G. scale) and reflect the middle to upper middle class as Leslie Paul points out (*The Payment and Deployment of the Clergy*, 1964). 'The ministry does constitute a social stratum. Its centre of gravity is middle to upper class. The centre of gravity is higher upper middle class to upper class for dignatories.' (*ibid.*, p. 114). Their education reflects a similar background with 33% coming from Public Schools and 62% from Grammar Schools. Nearly 80% have passed through University (1/3rd through Oxford or Cambridge) (cf. K. Jones *ibid.*) and so have developed an intellectual as well as a middle-class approach to life.

The Clergy on the Synod might not be completely representative of others in the church, but there is not a great deal of difference. Overall, the clergy give the impression of having a uniform background. Certainly entrance into the ministry encourages the same type of person to apply as in the past. Leslie Paul quoted the Fayers Heawood Analysis (1954–62) as suggesting that there was a strong bias towards Public School candidates in the church selection procedures, and although this might be less true today, the bias is still with us. Certainly the educational standards required still sift applicants so that it is mostly middle class men who are accepted. True it is now possible for older men without qualifications to be trained but there is still some reluctance to develop new forms of training for the ministry so that people from social classes 4 and 5 (semi and unskilled manual workers) are effectively excluded from that area of the church's life and leadership. Indeed such a choice of leaders has meant that at the congregational level, clergy leadership (whatever area the parish may be in) has been of a particularly middle class intellectual type. And that type of leadership has had a far greater affinity with the wealthy than with the poor. Not surprisingly church life flourishes in 'better off' areas, and not in areas of deprivation.

The third House in the General Synod comprises the laity. Here one would hope to find a wider cross section of backgrounds and experience. However, there is little difference between it and the other two houses. The 1970 Synod was described by the *Report of the Archbishops' Commission on Church and State* (para. 120, Proposal A) as 'dominated by the retired, the leisured, and the professional classes' with over two thirds being over 40 and one quarter being over 60 years old. By 1975 the Synod had changed to some extent but the same ethos prevailed. In terms of education over 30% had been to Public School and 54% to Grammar School; about 40% were graduates (a lower figure than for the clergy, and more of those went to universities other than Oxbridge).

In terms of occupation the Synod was still drawn mainly from the professions (class 1). There were about 16% from classes 2 and 3 (other managerial and salaried staff – non manual) but none from either class 4 or 5 (semi or unskilled manual workers). As Kathleen Jones has put it (*op. cit.*) 'The emphasis is not merely white collar, but white collar from the managerial and supervisory grades.' She goes on to point out that the traditional professions are heavily represented. 40% of the House were barristers, solicitors, teachers, university lecturers, doctors or engineers. The other significant grouping mentioned were such people as financial consultants, company directors, civil servant and local government officials. The House of Laity reflects the same pattern as the other two. Its members come from the middle to upper sector in society; through background and through their work. There is virtually no representation from poor or deprived areas.

So the General Synod reflects a similar social background to that of the bishops. All the dominant decision-makers in the Church of England come therefore from a very narrow sector of British society. This kind of emphasis ensures that the church remains closely connected with the middle and upper classes and as far removed as ever from the experience of the average working man in Britain, and from the real poverty that is present in particular areas of working class life.

Whatever area of church life is considered, the control by one small class of people is the same – the Church Commissioners, Church Property Boards and Finance Committees, the Doctrine and Liturgical Committees, the Pastoral Committees and Church Sites Committees, and the Diocesan Synods. At virtually all of these levels, policy decisions, practical decisions, future planning and strategy for the Church, theological discussion, all take place between people of one social background; namely that of the middle to upper classes.

Local congregations are not very different. Both the surveys of

Sillitoe (*Planning for Leisure*, 1969) and Wilmott and Young (*The Symmetrical Family*, 1975) endorse the point that church-going is far more prevalent amongst social classes 1 and 2 and non-manual class 3, than amongst the manual worker classes. Sillitoe suggests that a professional person may be three times more likely to attend church than a manual worker.

The size and geographical distribution of churches in England would certainly confirm this. There can be no doubt that the numerically strongest churches in Britain lie in the suburban/commuter belts surrounding the big cities. In comparison with these successful and thriving churches, the normal inner city or housing estate church is numerically weak, and financially struggling. The church therefore has consolidated itself well in the middle class and wealthier areas, whereas in the poorer and deprived areas it is struggling to stay alive. In describing this emphasis within the church, it is not being argued that wealth is to be found only in middle-class areas, and poverty only in working-class areas. Obviously the distribution of wealth is more complex than that. But what is being argued is that the church, being so predominantly middle class, is out of touch with working-class people and their culture in general (be they wealthy or poor by middle-class standards). At the same time it is also out of touch with poverty, and deprivation. The two issues are linked in that the heaviest concentration of poverty and deprivation is to be found in the inner city working class areas, of which the main body of the church has little real knowledge or experience.

With many churches in inner city areas desperately struggling to remain alive, why is it that numerically successful churches close by who could help out, do not? Indeed there is often very little interrelationship between churches of different sociological backgrounds. A simple example of this can be cited in South London where a struggling inner-city church appealed to three apparently thriving churches in a fashionable area, hardly 2 miles away, for personnel to help in the running of a community centre. Even though the need was serious no help was forthcoming. It would appear that many successful middle-class churches are afraid of their struggling fellow churches because they cannot cope with church life in a different social background, or with situations of poverty or deprivation; however much they may be aware of the situation of need, they appear to be frozen to inaction.

The church of the inner city is so overwhelmed with its massive overheads and the desperate needs of society around it that it either becomes a ghetto, or the congregation opts out and moves into the suburbs. In theory the church has a great concern for helping the poor, and has invested money and plant to do this, but in terms of personnel, of people who will live and work and serve in such areas, the Church's commitment is very weak.

The churches of the inner city and the council housing estates are also often very unrepresentative of the local population, and so even the churches in areas of deprivation do not reflect the local inhabitants. Instead such churches can very easily appear to contain social aspirers who would prefer to be middle class rather than working class. Indeed membership of the church can be seen by some as the way to enter middle-class respectability.

The church therefore seems to be most established within the middle to upper classes in society. Its strongest roots are among people who belong to classes 1, 2 and 3 (non manual) in the Registrar General's scale, but it fails to communicate with working class people, who make up the majority of the population; those described as class 4 and 5 (manual workers). Although it does have some contact with some of the real casualties of society through its commitment to social provision in deprived areas (e.g. community centres, youth clubs, dockland settlements, nursery groups, old people's day centres, etc.) it does not have a really widespread involvement in these areas. But these are, in essence, areas of service rather than areas where an indigenous church is established and growing.

Is the church pursuing a policy that will ultimately lead to a *totally* monochrome, 'one class' church? It appears that it is losing what little hold it previously had in urban areas, and the signs are that a major withdrawal of a recognised Christian presence and structure will occur if shortages of money and manpower (both clerical and lay) are not faced squarely. Such a withdrawal would only confirm what has always been suspected, that the church in areas of relative poverty and deprivation, is like a fish out of water.

Let us look at a final example of the church's relationship with wealth. It concerns the position of the church itself as an owner of wealth. It would be extremely difficult for it to take an unbiased view on the question of poverty and wealth because of its vested interests. The Church of England ranks only a little lower than the Royal Estate in the amount it owns, and an estimate in 1976 put the total wealth and property (at the price at which they are insured) of the Church of England at around £5,000m. The wealth of the Church Commissioners alone was estimated in 1979 as being £1028m. This wealth is of course made up mainly of property including church plant, agricultural land, housing estates, commercial and industrial estates, and some mineral rights and royalties; together with investments both in Government Stock and Equities. The Roman Catholic Church also holds a massive amount of wealth, and must be one of the richest property owners in Europe; though its holding in England is not so great. The nonconformist churches, being founded later, have not accumulated wealth to the same degree. Nevertheless they also have extensive ownership of property in the form of church plant and considerable investments.

The church has become alienated from the person of Christ, who owned nothing. He was able to identify with the poor because he was poor. In the same way the church's wealth requires it to identify with the rich because it is rich. It is doubtful if it has even begun to understand what it is like to be poor and powerless, for in order to have this understanding it is necessary to experience poverty and powerlessness oneself. Whereas Christ did so, the body of Christ today does not.

The wealth of the church is compromising in another way. Even if everyone agreed that the present state of society is one that encourages inequality and poverty, and ought from a Christian viewpoint to be radically changed, how could the church respond? If it was not so closely involved with the present system, it could bring real pressure to bear to change that system. But the wealth of the church is intricately bound up with the system itself so it depends on its continuation. Because the Church of England depends on interest from its invested wealth to continue the ministry, and so depends on the capitalist system even for the payment of the clergy, it cannot afford to question it. The church also owns a massive amount of property, some of which was obtained in medieval times by rather questionable methods. Would it therefore be interested in a redistribution of wealth or renunciation of property for the purposes of reducing inequality? There is no evidence at present that such a step would be encouraged.

Finally we need to note some ways in which the church, in its intellectual approach, stands on the side of wealth and power in society, rather than with those who are deprived of full humanity by society. The church is supporting the oppressor rather than the oppressed in its general attitudes, its silence, and by its general response to life.

a) *Dualism*

The church has accepted the concept of dualism – that life is divided into body and soul; matter and spirit and that these two aspects can be kept separate. But such a division leads to inadequate interpretations of the Gospel. For as long as faith can be divorced from reality the demand for the church to face the facts of human existence, is unheard. This division between sacred and secular has existed for hundreds of years. Centuries before Christ, Aristotle claimed that 'truth is incompatible with the condition of the slave,' but the society of that time was content to believe that truth had nothing to do with the sufferings of the four fifths of the population who happened to be slaves. Today, the church ought to be echoing Aristotle's words to Western society's élite; yet she does not, because she is trapped in the same dualism.

Christians are still confused by this approach, which puts faith in a separate compartment, so that the material realities of life are never challenged by the Christian message.

When faith is divorced from matter, when belief and behaviour are not applied to life, then it is no wonder that the church fails to relate its beliefs to the experiences of the vast majority of the world's population, who live only just above starvation level. The church is concerned only with what is palatable to her.

The dualistic approach still infiltrates the theology of the church as it has done in the past, and this stifles the growth of a concern for God's justice towards the poor and underprivileged. There still exists the idea that the realm of the Spirit is where God really is. Heaven, up above the bright blue sky, is thought of as being the ultimate utopia; and this earthly, material existence is the place of the devil's influence, to be escaped from as quickly as possible. This split, known as the Manichean heresy, still has a strong grip on the thinking of the church, and controls many of her day-to-day decisions, at both the local level, and within the hierarchy.

b) *The Individual and the Corporate*

Although Christians have been encouraged to help the poor and fight injustice as they meet it personally, there has been little awareness until recently that they ought also to be fighting against the *structures* that produce such poverty and injustice, and should be coming together as a body to speak out against these evils. Their corporate voice could have a far greater effect on society than that of individual Christians acting from time to time when their consciences are roused. This failure to act corporately may be partly due to the Protestant and evangelical tradition, which has tended to see the growth of God's Kingdom far more in terms of the conversion of individuals, than in changing the values of society to become more like the values of the Kingdom. It is argued that when more individuals become Christians, society will be changed. But would not the corporate church have far more weight in society if it were to speak out and work for the values of the Kingdom? Then Christianity would be seen to be truly on the side of the poor and the oppressed, and to be following the example of Christ's teachings. If the church were to recognise more fully the corporate nature of society and its own corporate nature within the body of mankind, then surely it would respond far more wholeheartedly to the evil and injustice in society and work more consistently for its elimination.

c) *Via Media*

Another way in which the church supports the wealthy rather than the poor is in its advocacy of the 'via media' as the answer to all problems. When faced with two divergent attitudes, on the one hand a Christian ideal, and on the other, the pragmatic attitude of society, the church has responded not by standing firm to the Christian ideal, but by seeking a path of compromise between the two. Perhaps an extreme example of this is the attitude of the church in South Africa toward 'apartheid'. With the exception of a few outstanding leaders who have now been deported, it has been content to disagree with the policy, and then make the best it can of the situation; rather than coming to the conclusion that there can be no compromise for a Christian on such a principle. For where black and coloured people are denied, by force, a fair share of their human heritage there can be no question of compromise from a biblical standpoint. The same could also be said of the oppression of political and religious dissidents in the Eastern Communist bloc, who are equally denied human rights. The church has done some remarkable work in slum areas, but consistently fails to attack the power structures that refuse to redistribute wealth on a fairer basis, so that the deprivation of the many is alleviated. By being satisfied with 'ambulance work', rather than preventive measures, the church is making a mockery of the Christian teaching about God's creation, man, and a just society. By easing the pain, rather than solving the problem, it is not declaring what the Gospel of Christ really is. It is making a mockery both of its own life, and of the Good News itself.

Let us look at three themes in the church's teaching which are interpreted in a way that waters down the Gospel. The theme of *reconciliation* is constantly recurring. We are all aware of the need for reconciliation between individuals in personal relationships, between groups of peoples in our society, and between employees and employers in industry. What then is the church's view? – it is one of compromise. Even on such a clear issue as the racism of the National Front, the church does not condemn the movement with one voice. Only one part of the church is speaking out against it. When protest rallies are held, they are poorly supported by church congregations. Even on such issues, where Christian principles are clearly abused, the church still declines to speak out clearly. Reconciliation is seen as finding common ground between two opposites.

However such a view of reconciliation is not biblical. It is very far from the way Jesus and the New Testament writers saw it. As Jose Bonino has pointed out (*Revolutionary Theology Come of Age*, p. 121), reconciliation in the Bible does not mean just ignoring or explaining away a contradiction; it means its effective removal. Jesus' attitude to evil is a case in point. He did not attempt to play it down or compromise on it, but left no doubt that it was wrong and was not acceptable to God. Then he went on to offer an alternative that was not *conciliatory*, but was a way of *reconciling* man to God. He died on the cross to break the power of evil, and gave up his life to defeat evil and offer a new way of life to anyone who wished to follow him and so be reconciled to God. He confronted evil and defeated it decisively. There was no compromise, or allowing the old ways to live together with the new. New wine, Jesus claimed, demanded new wineskins. So today Christ's 'New Age' cannot compromise, or co-exist with the old. His values are quite different; that difference will produce confrontation and conflict, not compromise. So the church's view of reconciliation can be seen as a perversion of the biblical truth. The church favours *conciliation* rather than *reconciliation*; it seeks peace at all costs, rather than the New Society.

Then there is the theme of *conflict*. Conflict is so often viewed as the opposite to order, and order is so often accepted as right, and 'Christian'. One of the results of the church's failure to be critical of society is that it accepts an unjust order. What happens when conflict, and even violence, need to be used to eliminate such injustice? Are there not times when order is wrong and conflict is required? Conflict can be seen as a positive weapon to achieve justice. It can be part of man's growing process. It can help society to develop. It need not necessarily be negative. On the whole, however, the church fails to view conflict positively. However serious the injustice may be, it does everything in its power to avoid conflict and violence. But this is not the biblical view. There are clear areas in the Bible where conflict is seen by God as necessary for eliminating evil and injustice, and for forwarding God's plan for his creation and his people.

It was used at the time of the Exodus and later to establish God's chosen people, and to eradicate idolatry amongst them. The eighth-century prophets came into conflict with the established order, when they attacked injustice. Jesus himself lived a life that involved conflict time and time again, with people and principles that opposed his 'new kingdom'. He unhesitatingly attacked those who oppressed others on religious grounds (the Pharisees) and on political or financial grounds (the Temple authorities and the money changers). In the Bible conflict and even violence are used as an acceptable 'means to break out of conditions (slavery, vengeance, arbitrariness, oppression, lack of protection, usurpation) that leave a man ... or people unable to be and act as a responsible agent ... in relation to others, to things, to God' (J. Bonino, *op. cit.* p. 118). But this attitude to conflict, is not the one taken by the church at present. Far more value is placed on the idea of peace coming from the preservation of order (regardless of the form that the order takes) and therefore the discouragement of conflict, rather than on peace coming from justice being done in a particular situation, which may well involve conflict. God is certainly concerned about peace, but he is concerned also about the *quality* of peace. And it would seem that for God's peace to be achieved in this world, conflict is required. The church lacks this concern for the quality of peace; it is satisfied to compromise with evil, and injustice rather than to confront it, as Jesus so clearly did. The conflict between Jesus and the demonic powers in so many people whom he healed, is not continued in the church's attitude to similar demonic behaviour by those in power, and by the wealthy élite of today.

Almsgiving is another theme which shows how uncommitted the church is to the poor. The word is often seen as meaning what the church gives to other people – particularly the poor. Such giving is seen as a charitable act, done by people of reasonable means to alleviate the suffering of people in need. Such gifts are given to show that the concern is there even if it is not possible to help the person any further.

However, if we look at the original biblical meaning of the word, we find that the present day understanding of the term has watered down the original meaning and given it a very easy and comfortable significance. For as Jose Miranda has pointed out (*Marx and the Bible*, pp. 14 ff) the original biblical understanding of the term is not acts of charity done by God's followers, but rather acts of justice. To 'give alms' in biblical terms is *'to do justice'* (cf. Prov. 10: 2, Dan. 4: 44, Mt. 6: 1–2). This biblical attitude is not concerned about giving a little from a surplus, an act that just alleviates some of the misery and at the same time cleanses the conscience of the giver.

The Bible sees almsgiving as a way in which God's followers can do something for a person in need, that will bring greater justice to his situation. The term is concerned, not only with the alleviation or reduction of suffering, but with its eradication. To be satisfied with alleviation and to have no concern for the eradication of the cause of suffering, does not take seriously the true meaning of the word. It is an example of a watered-down approach to Christian behaviour; a middle of the road approach, that does a little bit to help the sufferers but is careful not to tread on the toes of the powerful and wealthy by taking the issue too seriously.

Our conclusion therefore must be that the church is following a devious pattern. It is accepting poverty and injustice and their causes uncritically, without assessing them from a biblical and Christian standpoint. The church is far too often the mirror image of society instead of being an alternative way of life as Jesus envisaged when he inaugurated his new Kingdom. And as we shall see in the next chapter it is perpetuating attitudes that have been present ever since the time of the Emperor Constantine in Rome.

CHAPTER THREE

The Church, the Elite and Poverty in History

The identification of the church with the rulers of society down the ages has been a major factor in determining its present image. By forgetting the example of Christ who stood beside the poor and outcast all his life, the church has destroyed the essence of the gospel and weakened its expression and witness. We must begin, however, where the liaison first emerges in Rome in Constantine's rule.

Structures – Traditional or Biblical

One of the most influential steps in determining the shape and expression of our present church was taken unobtrusively in Rome during the fourth century. It was a simple step, yet one of devastating significance which has resulted in a church that finds it hard to follow Christ's example, because of its own structure. As F. Houtart describes it (*The Church and Revolution*, pp. 339 ff) the church rather than developing a biblical structure of communion in all its internal relationships, developed instead a hierarchical structure similar to the Roman pattern. So instead of going back to its revealed beginnings, to find suitable patterns to develop, the church took the traditional structure with all its shortcomings and attempted to sacralise it. This meant that the church became, not so much a communion of people, with one belief in Christ, but rather a pyramidal structure, that had a head like the Emperor – the Pope – and then various levels of officials (the bishops and priests), down to the mass of ordinary members of society (the lay people in each congregation).

The sacralising of the traditional social structure, led to a great variety of decisions which now affect every part of the life of the church. Though not wrong in itself this approach often led the church away from the example of Christ and crucial biblical principles. As well as taking on a hierarchical structure, the church also took on many of the judicial, administrative, and authoritarian patterns of the Roman state. For instance, it was at this time that the priest began to be seen as in some way superior to his congregation, and that bishops were accepted as state, as well as church, officials, and were sometimes paid by the state. The church accepted also some aspects of Roman culture: their clothes as vestments for the liturgy, their style of architecture for their church buildings, their symbols of prestige and titles (cf. *A History of Religion East and West*, Trevor Ling, p. 181).

The church even went on to accept the Empire's system of 'gentle persuasion' when it came to dissidents, using force to silence and suppress unorthodox views. They even learnt to use force in their role as missionaries just as the Romans coerced various tribes into becoming part of their Empire. Such attitudes were a travesty of what Jesus envisaged when he told his disciples to go to the ends of the earth to preach the Gospel. So the church modelled itself on a social and cultural pattern that it did not sufficiently scrutinise or criticise. Ever since, it has tended to conform to and accept the dominant social structure of the day, without considering whether this is right or wrong, supporting, and even using a society that displays distinctly anti-Christian principles, as the Dutch Reformed Church does in South Africa.

The adoption of Roman patterns for its internal structures, was followed by the English church as well as by the church in Rome. The decision for the English church came in AD 664 at the Synod of Whitby. Before that time there were two distinct expressions of Christianity in England; the Celtic and the Roman. The Roman followed the pattern brought from Rome and was responsible for the conversion of some parts of England. However, the greater part of England had been converted through the Celtic Church which was far less organised than the Roman, and in some ways chaotic. Yet it did have an incredible zeal, love and commitment that enabled it to spread the gospel like wildfire through itinerant monks and preachers who left their monasteries and travelled everywhere to preach the word. Their faith was a spontaneous, and exciting one, springing from a vital Christian experience. However, at Whitby, a decision had to be made as to which church was to become *the* church in England, and the decision went in favour of Rome. Certainly there were positive gains as a result of this decision; but at the same time, the English church accepted the mistakes already made in Rome and lost much of what was vital, living and biblical from the Celtic influence, an influence that had been the major factor in the original conversion of the English peoples.

The Church and the Powerful

From the time of Constantine onward there was a close relationship between the spiritual and temporal leadership. Although this was intended for mutual benefit the two sides were sometimes in conflict. During the times when the Pope was in ascendancy the liaison suited the church well. But when the Emperor wished to control the power of the church then the latter suffered severely.

The issue of 'investiture' in the time of the Emperor Charlemagne, demonstrates the problem. While the church held authority over the Emperor all was well. The issue was: should the Emperor and his overlords have the power to elect the Pope, the Bishops and other clergy, or should this remain the right of the church alone?

Charlemagne was the first important temporal leader to exert such authority which was contrary to the earlier principle set up by Cyprian, of Bishops being elected by the people, and consecrated by another Bishop. Subsequently Emperors and their overlords tended to appoint their choice of Bishop, and often their choice was the man who bid the highest sum of money for the post. However, in 1075 Pope Gregory VII decreed that no temporal authority could elect a man into an ecclesiastical benefice (including the Papacy). This caused a massive political controversy that raged until 1122. The church demanded that she should be granted autonomy in the appointment of her own leadership; while the secular leadership did not want to lose the power that it had over the church.

A compromise was reached; the church was to have the spiritual and the Emperor the temporal jurisdiction over appointments. But the issue was never truly settled, and the principle behind it was still one that consistently proved controversial. For the liaison between the church and temporal rulers, while being beneficial to both sides at times, also showed up the very different purposes and aims of the two parties. It became clear that the church when it held true to its faith, was not prepared to be limited or controlled by secular rulers who had other aims and methods. Yet at the same time it became clear that much as the church wanted autonomy, it could not extricate itself from the influence of the temporal powers. It became against its will a servant of two masters.

From 1066 to 1300 a similar battle was fought between the church and the English kings and their barons. The Norman kings wished to keep control of the English church by appointing their own Bishops and clerics whilst the church wanted that authority for itself. William II blatantly sold bishoprics to the highest bidder, and both Henry II and John tried to dominate and control the church as though it were part of their temporal kingdom. Although it temporarily retained hold of its own affairs, by 1300 power over the issue of elections had passed to the monarch (cf. *Cathedral and Crusade*, p. 217). In 1351 and 1353 this was further enforced by Richard II in the Statutes of Provisers and Praemunire which forbade the church the right to appeal to the Pope against appointments made by the king.

So the liaison between the church and the temporal rulers was one that ultimately benefited the rulers rather than the church. It was granted considerable influence; it was endowed with massive wealth, and land. But it gained such benefits at the expense of its own freedom. For its leadership in the main was appointed by the temporal rulers so that it would follow the demands of those rulers. The Church lost its independence and ended up serving two masters instead of one. (Even today the government has the last word in appointing the bishops of the Church of England.)

This oversight of the church by temporal rulers was of course not just limited to the kings and their appointment of bishops. For at every level the temporal overlords exerted their authority over the church. Just as the kings appointed bishops, the nobility appointed other bishops and abbots, and the local landowner appointed his cleric to his church in the village. The church like the bakery and the farm was a place where he set the man who would serve his interests best.

The church had become engulfed in the feudal system: 'consciously or more often unconsciously she had committed the mistake of linking her fortunes too closely with prevailing sociological factors' (*Cathedral and Crusade*, H. Daniel Rops, p. 170). The bishops became feudal overlords and acted just like other barons. Ecclesiastical appointments became endowed with land, serfs and power, and were hence sought after just as much as the secular positions by those who wanted power and wealth. So, the church at every level lost its independence of action by its acceptance of outside secular control, and by its involvement in the feudal system that, at that time, dominated society.

So, too the demands of the Gospel began to take second place to placating the élite and the rulers, and living at peace with them.

a) *Power bringing wealth and corruption*

One of the most striking effects of the church's close relationship with the powerful in English society, has been its accumulation of wealth during particular periods. Proof of this have been the continual attempts, both successful and unsuccessful, to relieve it of such wealth. However, there is another issue concerning this wealth and power; the profound effect it has always had on the life of the church, as a *corrupting* influence. To illustrate this point, let us look at one particular period of English church history.

From the thirteenth century to the sixteenth century, the church's wealth grew from approximately one quarter of the land and consequent wealth of England, to what was estimated, just before the Dissolution of the Monasteries, at around one third of the total national wealth. For one body within society to have such wealth seems impossible today. At one time it made a considerable impact on society, and its attitude toward the church, and very strong anti-clerical feelings developed, mainly because of this wealth, and the corruption it brought. Such material riches stand opposed to the life, teaching and witness of the founder of the church.

The wealth of the church gradually increased during this period in a variety of ways. There were tithes and taxes, income from wills and endowments, such as land and buildings, by rich benefactors. As well as receiving these gifts at death, the church also received an income through penances leading to the granting of absolution. With the regular income from the land owned, both from farm production, rent, and even in later times massive royalties from coal production, the church was 'big business' (comparable only with the state).

The corruption started at the top, with many of the church leaders being the richest men in the country. Cardinal Wolsey at one time rivalled Henry VIII in wealth; and although he is an extreme example, there were plenty of other leading churchmen who became exceedingly rich, as they were in a position to manipulate church funds for their own gain. At the same time they often worked more for the state and for themselves, than for the church to which they owed their position. The richer clergy, and very many within the monasteries, were able to live opulent lives. Rich churchmen delegated their spiritual responsibilities to clerks, many of whom were underpaid, and absenteeism and pluralism were rife. Corruption was a plague in the life of the church. William Langland in *Piers*

THE CHURCH, THE ELITE AND POVERTY

Plowman talks of Sloth the parson, who could not read a line of a book after being in the parish thirty years. Wyclif spent much of his life denouncing the abuses of wealth and power that were so much a part of church life, as had the Early Fathers in the fourth century and later some of the monastic orders in the twelfth and thirteenth centuries. During Constantine's time, St. Basil and St. John Chrysostomos were outstanding in their commitment to the poor. This was true also of the Waldensians, the 'poor men of Lyons and Lombardy' and of some of the orders such as the Franciscans, *[after St. Francis of Assisi]* all of whom consistently lived lives of poverty, and stood in solidarity beside the poor and against exploitation by the wealthy in both church and secular society. The great revolt of 1381 was partly caused by the wealth and opulence of the church, at a time when the mass of people were starving. It would seem that the Archbishop of Canterbury, who was also Chancellor of England, was responsible for allowing much of the current massive poverty and oppression (cf. *A History of the Church of England* – J. Moorman, p. 118). And by Henry VIII's time, it was clear that everyone was envious of the position of the monks in their monasteries. Gone was the ascetic life of earlier times. Many monks enjoyed the good life. It was because of such corruption, that Henry's move to dissolve the monasteries was not altogether unpopular.

It is hard for us to envisage wealth and corruption on such a scale today. Yet this was what the church was really like. Only the wealthy in church and society failed to see the anomaly between its ideals and its practice. Of course that period was an extreme example in the life of the church, and much of the wealth came to an end with the dissolution of the monasteries. But even after the dissolution, the church still held and gradually increased its huge wealth of land and treasures. So the circle of wealth and corruption remained.

b) *Power bringing alienation from Human Experience*

There has been a more serious and subtle failure than material corruption. The church has become identified with the rich and powerful, and *alienated* from the poorer and weaker members of society. *[How do we overcome this? Is it even possible?]* It has failed to appreciate the reality of life experienced by those who are receiving less than their fair share of their God given, human rights. The church is now unable to appreciate what it is like to be dominated, to be led, to be controlled. Having taken sides, it is now unable to make an objective assessment of what is happening to society. If the Christian faith is to have any real effect on society, this assessment that was an intrinsic part of Jesus' message is essential; for before he was able to offer a solution, he first had to assess the basic state of man. So the fact that the church is wedded to one part of society, both historically and currently makes it impossible for it to comprehend, or identify with anyone who is not part of that privileged élite. Evidence of such failure will be given from one period in history. Let us look at the church's alienation during the period of the Agricultural and Industrial Revolutions.

This period highlights the relationship between the peasant/unskilled or semi-skilled artisan, and the squire or employer. New factors were introduced into the relationship, that stretched it to its limits. It is one of the most glaring examples in English history of the exploitation of the working man, both economically and politically, to the advantage of the landed gentry, mill owners, and capital holders. How did the church respond to such a situation of need? The economic and political pressures were intense, forcing the working man into extreme deprivation, but the church on the whole seemed unable to realise what was happening. Its faith should have called it to stand beside those who were being deprived, and to speak with and for them. But although there were exceptions which will be considered carefully, the church as a whole was out of touch with the mass of English working people, and was instead both élitist and remote.

An important sociological change in England started around the mid-eighteenth century. A new system of agriculture was gradually superseding the established pattern. The main factor in this was the enclosure of land, which had been taking place since the fifteenth century, but which increased in intensity until nearly all lands were enclosed by the 1840's. Ownership of property in the rural areas hence became concentrated in a far smaller and more wealthy class, to the deprivation of the small independent farmer. Some of this came about through routine sale and purchase of land, but some was forced through by private acts of Parliament, put through by people who knew how to manipulate the House of Commons. Many of the smaller landowners could not afford to enclose their land, and so were bought out and some became pauperised, and had to travel the roads for work. The small man lost his rights to the growing wealthy élite, and also lost a share of the increasing wealth accruing from the land.

At the same time as the Agricultural revolution took place, society was being transformed by what we now know as the Industrial Revolution. The growth of technology was a major cause: the use of the steam mill, the expansion of the cotton industry, and the

THE CHURCH, THE ELITE AND POVERTY 57

possibilities which developed from the combination of coal and iron, to produce steel, encouraged the transformation. Added to these changes was the huge increase in population in England, at the beginning of the nineteenth century, and its concentration in great industrial conurbations. The situations was made more complex by political events. The end of the eighteenth century in Europe was a time when the 'liberty tree' was being planted. The working man was arising to demand his rights as a human being. The French Revolution affected not only France, but also brought either fear, or encouragement, to England. Political unrest grew here too, fuelled by the Wesleyan revival, and the growing industrial discontent. The time was ripe for dynamic change, and a radical restructuring of society. There was a spectacular increase in wealth since the change in manufacturing methods and the scale on which manufacture was carried on, brought the chance of making huge sums of money very quickly. This was seized by those who had capital to invest in the new methods of production. However, the new wealth created by technology, was not fairly shared, and while the employer was getting much richer, the new industrial employee, although earning a better wage than could be obtained for rural work, was paying dearly for this small financial benefit by having to live in the most appalling and degrading surroundings. A vivid picture of the plight of the industrial worker of this time is found in Mrs. Gaskell's *Mary Barton*.

The new manufacturing élite as well as the wealthy gentry, were helped in retaining their position by the political situation at the turn of the century. Instead of reforms being achieved in the 1790's, through the influence of the French Revolution and Napoleonic Wars, these events brought about an alliance between the old aristocracy and the new industrialists, which effectively put back the prospect of reform for nearly forty years (cf. Thompson – *The Making of the English Working Class*, p. 197). During this time, wages were kept down, workmen were not allowed to meet together, and there were repeals of a number of acts that protected wages, apprenticeships, and working conditions in industry (e.g. The Combination Acts). Private acts were also used at this time, as we have seen, to bring about enclosures, and force small farmers to sell out. The corn Laws brought in after the Napoleonic Wars, protected the price of corn for the wealthy landowners, and at the same time sent the cost of bread to a level that the ordinary family could hardly afford. The 'Speenhamland Act' of 1795 when bread prices were already high, had the effect of enabling farmers to peg their workers' wages, and have them subsided by the rates. This meant that the working man became a pauper, and the farmer increased his corn profits. In the huge cotton towns the local councils were very slow to show any response to the increased needs of the expanding population, and allowed living conditions to deteriorate.

It was during this period that the worker began to be seen much more as an 'instrument', than as a human being. The feudal interdependence of master and man was eroded; there was not even any interest in giving a man a 'just' wage, but only the lowest wage that could be enforced. The worker had become solely a means of production for his master.

The Industrial Revolution had brought about a crucial change in the nature of English society by dramatically intensifying exploitation. As the worker began to express himself and fight against economic pressure, he began to be exploited politically as well. Both politics and the law were used to stop him alleviating or bettering his position. The late eighteenth and early nineteenth centuries were times of extreme exploitation of humanity by both a new and an old élite, determined to cling to their advantages.

However, as Thompson points out (*The Making of the English Working Class*, p. 204) we cannot lay the blame for each hardship of the Industrial Revolution upon the 'masters'; or upon '*laissez-faire*'. Historians have been at pains to point out that there are many other reasons for the difficulties. The markets fluctuated incessantly, hurting the employee more than the employer. It was a time of industrial 'take off', when all the infrastructures of society were being re-built. There were pressures as a result of the population explosion. Although at great cost, the work force of that period was laying the foundations of an industrial structure that was to be enjoyed by Britain for over one hundred years.

It is still not possible to avoid the charge of exploitation. In the 1840's the country was much wealthier than 100 years previously, and that wealth was firmly held by an industrial and rural élite, who lived in considerable opulence, while living conditions for the working man had scarcely improved at all. So with all the extenuating circumstances, with all the help from 'hindsight', it is still not possible for anyone to forget the pressures put on the working man between 1750 and 1850.

In the mid-eighteenth century the church, in general, was totally out of touch with everyday life. It was dominated by the Latitudinarianism that was to colour church attitudes for a long time to come. Gradually, however, changes began to be seen in the growth of Methodism, Evangelical humanitarianism, and ultimately Christian Socialism. Let us look therefore at these various expressions of church life, and their attitudes towards the vast changes and exploitation in society.

The Latitudinarian spirit was probably the strongest influence in the church of the time, because it was so fully established. It permeated every aspect of church life. It stood for reasonableness in the interpretation of doctrine, and in the practical matters of life, and assumed that the status quo was right, thus allowing the church to identify with the richer, rather than the poorer, people in society. There was an emphasis on the procuring of wealthy livings, and worldly advantage that started with the bishops, and went right down to the local clergyman. Even the village parson would be at pains to keep in with the landowners and the squire (c.f. G. M. Trevelyan – *English Social History* p. 358). The ministry of both the bishop, and the parson, was geared to speak to the powerful rather than the poor. As in earlier days, pluralism, absenteeism, and sinecures were still the order of the day, so that corruption was very real. Many church leaders saw themselves as figures in secular life, rather than ministers of the Body of Christ. All these attitudes led to the church being completely out of touch with the working man, both at the start of the revolutionary period, and also well into it.

The French Revolution and the Jacobin influence far from liberalising the church served to strengthen its position behind the wealthy ruling class, against the newly emergent working class. The church in France had lost so much of its power and wealth during the Revolution, that the church here was very concerned lest it should suffer the same experience. When Tom Paine published *The Rights of Man* in 1791, the church leaders were among the first to condemn such subversive thinking. So the weight of the church's influence was used to slow down the awakening of humanitarian ideals. Witness its attitude to the 1832 Reform Bill. In spite of the reforming influence of Methodism it was still totally committed to *laissez-faire*, and the High Tory Party, and against any kind of reform within society. With regard to the Reform Bill it was said of the church 'there is but one class opposed ... with anything like unanimity – the clergy of the Church of England'. The bishops in the House of Lords were against the Bill: twenty-one voted against, and only two for it. No wonder that during this period, there was intense anti-clerical feeling: particularly against the higher ranks.

It was during this time that non-conformism and later the movements of evangelical humanitarianism arose. How much influence these movements had on the church as a whole is hard to assess; it still stood firmly against the Reform Bill. Let us look in more detail at the growth of nonconformism, for it is from this movement rather than the established church that there came a genuine Christian response to the upheavals of the Industrial and Agricultural Revolution.

The thinking behind Methodism and the Evangelical Revival was complex. Here was a religious movement that truly affected and converted the working class man, even in the depths of his misery. Methodism had a great following in the working class, in the industrial cities, and influenced even the radical thinkers. Wesley's preaching had a profound influence. The class meetings, and the community spirit that developed within them enabled the movement to grow impressively, and the working man to grow in self confidence. The movement showed that working men could organise themselves, and that leaders could emerge from their midst. Christianity was seen to be concerned about a human being's physical welfare and men taught that God hated the evils of exploitation. The movement was responsible for the thinking behind Kilham's *The Progress of Liberty* (1795). There were many respects in which the Methodists offered new and radical thinking.

Methodism, however, was a religion that had not only many working class members, it was also the religion of many of the new 'bourgeoisie' of the time – it was in fact more a religion *for* the poor, than a religion *of* the poor. It was started by middle class men, and although it was taken up by the working man, the middle class influence remained. There was always tension between the more autocratic Wesleyan leadership, and the later more democratic local lay leadership that emerged. Having supporters from both the middle class, and the working class, the successful mill owner, as well as his workmen, led to a theology that was far less radical than many people would like to believe. The New Connexion of Kilham, and its radical thinking was not perpetuated. Wesley himself had preached – 'Blessed are the poor' – but the insistence that the poor were of value in the sight of God and man gave way to an acceptance of their earthly condition. Certainly there was a concern for those who were suffering; but the idea that the poor should actively demand changes began to recede. And as Thompson points out (*op. cit.* pp. 388–9) there was an element in the growth of Methodism which suggested, that when political reform was obstructed spiritual growth took its place. In other words a place in God's heaven was the next best satisfaction if present miseries could not be avoided.

This other side of Methodism gradually led to a kind of corruption by wealth and position which even Wesley foresaw in the early days. For the Methodists, being committed to discipline and diligence, soon began to make their way up in the world. Soon those

THE CHURCH, THE ELITE AND POVERTY

who were workers found themselves more and more in positions of power and wealth because of their strong work ethic. And as is so often the case, wealth began to blind those people to the needs of the industrial worker. As bourgeois values began to predominate in Methodism, the more radical ideas of Christian justice were diluted. In fact this 'toning down' of the potentially radical nature of Christianity by the Methodist movement, has given rise to Halevy's famous thesis, that Methodism actually prevented revolution in England during the 1790's (Halevy – *A History of the English People in 1815*). He suggests that, rather than encouraging the working man to demand his rights, alongside Tom Paine, and many other radical thinkers, Methodism actually had the opposite effect.

So we must not give too much weight to the idea that the positive values of Methodism offset the response of Latitudinarianism towards the sufferings of the working man during this period. Methodism *seemed* to respond to the needs of the deprived, and yet, when it came to real emancipation, and Jesus' idea of a religion *of* the poor, rather than *for* the poor, then Methodism like so many other movements gave in to the wealthy and powerful, quickly forgetting what it is really like to be poor, deprived, oppressed and exploited.

A movement, that has always been seen as having a real Christian understanding of, and active passion for the needs of the poor was the *evangelical humanitarian* group founded by Wilberforce, Shaftesbury and others: and the Clapham Sect.

The humanitarian influence which grew from the work of the Clapham Sect members, had a very real effect on both church life and middle class attitudes of the time. The leaders, including Wilberforce, Venn, Stephen, Thornton, Macaulay, and later Shaftesbury, committed themselves to a life of piety, and very real humanitarian concern. They achieved a great deal for human rights, often at a time when it was very unpopular to do so, and led the way towards a growing change of heart amongst the middle classes, no mean feat in itself. Their concern included the abolition of slavery, the education of the poor, and the establishing of hospitals and other philanthropic institutions on behalf of the poor. They attacked also the barbarous nature of the law, and the appalling state of the prisons. Their work led to the support and encouragement of Shaftesbury's factory legislation.

However, although we acknowledge the influence of this humanitarian group which contrasts so markedly with the traditional Established Church/High Tory/*laissez-faire* alliance of the day, (and indeed seemed to work better with the radical freethinkers like Bentham, than their supposed Christian counterparts in the church,) we must examine their attitudes carefully and not credit them with more than their work deserves. Although they were full of humanitarian zeal, they worked for the poor, rather than *with* them. They were completely committed to making the life of the poor easier, yet they were quite happy to accept that the poor were the poor, and saw no reason why they shouldn't continue to remain so. Wilberforce, Shaftesbury, and the rest were upper class people, who believed that God had put people into classes, and that it was therefore wrong to make any changes that would upset the wealth or class structure. Wilberforce expounded his 'grand law of subordination', and suggested how the poor should be treated. He believed 'that their more lowly path has been allotted to them by the hand of God; that it is their part faithfully to discharge its duties, and contentedly to bear its inconveniences; that the present state of things is very short; that the objects about which worldly men conflict so eagerly are not worth the contest' (W. Wilberforce – *A Practical View of the Prevailing Religious System of Professed Christians*, 1797, pp. 405–6). Theirs were attempts to alleviate the *extremes* of deprivation, rather than a determined effort to redress the imbalance, which had been created or at least aggravated, by the Industrial Revolution. They led the way in reducing the amount of suffering, but they were still not able to see that its basic cause was man's inhumanity to man. That task was once more to be left to secular thinkers, and activists. Christian thinkers were still too dominated by their middle class and upper class heritage to be able truly to appreciate the depth of suffering, and the need for its elimination. Because they were the beneficiaries of the economic order they could not see how such a structure in society, with all the suffering that it entailed for the masses, was an abomination to the God whom they worshipped.

c) *Theological Support for Identification with the powerful*

Throughout English history there have been religious ideas that have encouraged the church, either consciously or unconsciously, in its identification with the powerful and richer classes. These ideas have either directly brought wealth into the hands of the church, or have justified the way in which Christians always seemed to move from poverty to wealth and never vice versa. In the process Jesus' teaching on wealth and possessions has been undermined. One of the greatest influences on Christian thinking in the Middle Ages was the people's attitude towards death. People were very concerned about death, and what would happen afterwards, so the church was in a very strong position when it proclaimed that if people followed

THE CHURCH, THE ELITE AND POVERTY

Christ's way i.e. the teaching of the church, then they would all receive eternal life. The church became in effect a purveyor of immortality; if you wanted a life after death, you had to keep in favour with the church; it was offering a place in heaven to people in return for 'services rendered'. The church was prepared to offer peace of mind to those with money – as D. M. Stenton suggests (*English Society in the Early Middle Ages*, pp. 203–4 in Pelican History of England Vol. 3) 'From one point of view the whole vast organisation of the Medieval Christian Church can be regarded as a result of man's fear of eternal damnation and his desire for eternal bliss. It was for this that rich men gave land to the religious, who paid for it by prayer on behalf of their patrons. There was a direct simplicity about the relationship between God and man, an element of bargain, a hint of the market place.' This teaching and practice led during the period between the Norman and Tudor kings to a massive accumulation of wealth by the church on account of the immortality it was able to hand out as God's representative. The church was able to hold on to that wealth only by having the same power over the kings, who (other than John and, of course, Henry VIII), didn't dare to incure the wrath of the church, and hence God, for very long. So it was to a very real degree a theological issue, that was used by the church as an instrument to gain wealth and power, and also to keep it.

The fear of death, and the desire for eternal life continued to be a central issue in popular thinking for a long time. During the Industrial Revolution we find the church using the same issue, but in a different way, and with different results. The Revivalist religion of the Methodist and Evangelical movement at that time put a very high priority on eternal life. Worldly needs were seen as secondary to man's spiritual needs, and his life after death with God. Thus religion became 'other worldly', as Christians became far more concerned about their life after death, than about the conditions of living in this world. This encouraged the church not to take too seriously the exploitation and suffering around it. Certainly there were exceptions to the rule, such as the Clapham Sect, Kilham's New Connexion and the more politically orientated Methodists. Yet even so, this attitude did much to encourage Christians not to be concerned in reforming this world, which was regarded as less important than the next.

To many Christians, the classes of society were believed to have been pre-ordained by God. Wilberforce (who was probably far more enlightened than most Christians of his day) seems to imply that it was God's plan to have a rich and a poor class; and that just as the rich were supposed to accept the position they were placed in, so too the poor were expected to accept the limitations of their position. They were to be submissive to their superiors, and accept that God made some people superior to others. They were to accept the decisions of the powerful, and the laws of the state as being totally right and acceptable in God's eyes. They were discouraged from making any suggestions, as to how the laws could in any way be changed for the better. They were called to be disciplined in their way of life, accepting obediently the advice of their superiors. They were also told emphatically about Jesus' teaching on the poor. This was interpreted to mean that it really was *blessed* to be poor. The poor would inherit a fantastic life after death. They were called to accept the present sufferings of poverty, because their reward in heaven would then be even greater. (This was even used as an excuse for farmers not putting up their labourers' wages!!) It was this kind of teaching, already present in the Established church in the late eighteenth century, that affected later Methodist attitudes, and reduced considerably the possibility of revolution during the period of the French Revolution.

Another religious idea that was reinforced during the period was the so-called protestant work ethic. It first became prominent with the Methodists, during the later days of Wesley. Wesley saw that Christians were called to live simply, eat frugally, work hard, live disciplined lives and spend little. This work ethic often resulted in Christians becoming very rich. This led easily to the corruption of the original Christian ideal. Wesley put it like this. 'Religion must necessarily produce both industry and frugality, and these cannot but produce riches. But as riches increase, so will pride, anger, and the love of the world.... How then is it possible that Methodism, that is, a religion of the heart, though it flourishes now as a green bay tree, should continue in this state? For Methodists in every place grow diligent and frugal; consequently they increase in goods. Hence they proportionately increase in pride, in anger, in the desires of the flesh, the desires of the eyes, and the pride of life. So although the form of religion remains, the spirit is swiftly vanishing away.' What Wesley described is exactly what happened in Methodism after his death, and has continued in protestantism ever since. It can for instance still be seen today, in the way in which Christians living in the inner cities, when they become converted, soon move out to more pleasant surroundings. The corruption by wealth which leads from the acquiring of wealth is something that the church has never been able to counteract. There seems to be no Christian prohibition against making money and although there is plenty of advice as to how to spend it and how to value the possessions that can be obtained with it that advice is rarely heard.

Vested Interests and their influence on the Church

So we see that the church in England has never been a 'law unto itself'. It has not been able to respond directly to the Word of the Gospel. The church has not been its own keeper, because it has been controlled by the vested interests that have helped it reach the position that it is now in.

The influence of these vested interests upon the church, means that it has never been able to respond directly to the demands of its head – Jesus Christ. It has always had to look behind it, before making a decision. For were the church to speak without consideration for those vested interests, it might have lost the financial support that has always enabled it to prosper, or it might have been silenced, and stopped from speaking out, by the power that such interests have had over the church itself. Today the church is in a similar position to the British Government, which was recently asked to make an investments embargo on South Africa. To do so, would mean considerable financial and practical losses, for the sake of a moral or spiritual principle. The cost of such a decision is so high that, without incredible pressure, it will not be made by the British Government or by the church.

But these vested interests also involve the individuals within the church. The decisions of the church have been made by individuals, many of them from the wealthy and powerful classes, who are dependent on the present system for their wealth, power and position. Were these interests to be questioned, and attacked on Christian grounds, such individuals could be in danger of losing a great deal. They therefore, as individuals and as church leaders, have vested interests that they are unwilling to risk.

So both at a structural, and at the individual level, the church has been prevented from being the true Body of Christ. Its interests have kept it from responding to Christ's message to stand beside the poor. They have forced it to maintain a liaison with the powerful, and have prevented any real identification with or support of the poor, the outcasts, the oppressed and the exploited.

As we have looked down through history, we have seen how this link with the élite started, and how it developed. We have also seen the appalling results of such a link and the way in which people rejected the Christian faith, through no fault of the faith, but through the fault of the church's corruption by power and wealth.

These failures in the past are certainly appalling, and highly embarrassing. They are failures that need to be atoned for, in the present and future. Once having seen such failure, Christians of today will be called to repent of the sins of the past, and make radical restitution wherever possible.

But now we need to go back to the Bible to look afresh at what it has to say. We need to consider the biblical attitudes to wealth and poverty, to justice and oppression, to the élite and the poor. We need to consider biblical guidelines that could put the church on a far more Christian footing. We need to look for the basis of a biblical critique of society and biblical proposals for the way ahead. For the inadequacy of the capitalist system from a biblical standpoint does not in itself mean that Christians should support another of the prevailing political philosophies, such as socialism or Marxism, but rather that they should develop their own approach that is firmly rooted in biblical principles.

CHAPTER FOUR

Biblical Attitudes Towards the Poor and Oppressed

In the next two chapters we shall turn to the Bible seeking a truly Christian response to the state of wealth and poverty in national and international society. Then, as it becomes clear how divergent the church's behaviour has become from the biblical guidelines, we will need to go on to consider the various changes required for the church to return to the biblical norm.

We start therefore in this chapter by looking at the central issue – the biblical attitude towards the poor and oppressed. Rather than taking isolated incidents, I shall attempt to take themes that recur through the Old and New Testament. From the start we shall find that the Bible, unlike the church, takes an uncompromising stand on the issue. Throughout biblical history, although God's people turned one way and then the other, God's word has rung out clear, through the words and actions of God himself, through his leaders, his prophets, and then ultimately through Christ and his disciples. There is a distinct approach on the one hand, to wealth, power and materialism, and on the other towards those deprived of their God-given rights. I am particularly indebted to Jose Miranda, who has analysed the matter so clearly by his both scholarly and practical exegetical study of the subject (cf. *Marx and the Bible – A Critique of the Philosophy of Oppression*).

Knowledge of God and Justice

To begin our search for a truly Christian attitude towards wealth and poverty, we must see what it meant to the earliest followers of the faith, to 'know' God. What did 'knowing' God lead them to do in relation to wealth and poverty in the society in which they lived? The clearest communication of the theme which we can find is in the writings of Jeremiah and Hosea. To Jeremiah, to 'know' God meant to do justice to all men. He puts this clearly as he describes the difference between King Josiah and his son Shallum, who failed to live up to Josiah's example (Jeremiah 22: 13–16) 'Woe to him who builds his house by unrighteousness, and his upper rooms by injustice; who makes his neighbour serve him for nothing, and does not give him his wages; who says "I will build myself a great house with spacious upper rooms" and cuts out windows for it, panelling it with cedar, and painting it with vermilion. Do you think you are a king because you compete in cedar? Did not your father eat and drink and do justice and righteousness? Then it is well with him. He judged the cause of the poor and needy; then it is well. *Is not this to know me? says the Lord.*' Jeremiah saw that to know God, meant doing justice to the poor and needy. Josiah could be seen to know God because of his attitudes and actions towards the poor and needy. On the other hand, Shallum Josiah's son could not possibly know God, because he oppressed people for his own personal gain. Hosea expresses the same attitude, as he prophesies against evil practices in Israel, (Hos. 4: 1b–2). 'There is no faithfulness or kindness, and no knowledge of God in the land; there is swearing, lying, killing, stealing and committing adultery; they break all bounds and murder follows murder.' Such behaviour showed that the people did not even know God. It was not that they were forgetting their faith or backsliding; they simply did not know God. To these prophets therefore there was no division between a knowledge of God and doing justice to those in need. They saw them as synonymous. It was not a matter of a certain understanding of God leading on to certain behaviour. Doing justice was an intrinsic part of 'knowing' God which was not an intellectual activity, idea or belief but a total response. As Johannes Botterweck has put it (*Gott Erkennen* – Bonn, Peter Hanstein Verlag, 1951, p. 97) 'In the writings of the pre exilic prophets as well as in certain sections of the Wisdom literature, the knowledge of God means a religious/moral form of conduct of men towards Yahweh: to know God means to renounce sin and the worship of idols, to "return" to Yahweh and to "seek" for him to "depend" upon him and to "fear" him; it means to "practise live, justice, righteousness". He who knows God walks in his ways. Knowledge of God is active piety.' Indeed Botterweck goes even further when referring to

BIBLICAL ATTITUDES: THE POOR AND OPPRESSED

Josiah's attitudes: 'fraternal justice is for the king the sum total (or "essence") of the knowledge of God' (*op. cit.*, p. 45). In other words, there cannot be the slightest comprehension of God, without its being reflected in the believer's relationships with others and particularly in his attitude towards the poor and deprived.

Such a view of knowing God committed the prophets to standing clearly for justice, in a society that in many ways lacked it. It led them to speak out against injustices and against those who were perpetrating them. They made that stand, regardless of whom they confronted. They condemned the extremes of wealth that enforced poverty on others. It was clear to them that to identify with those in need, included speaking against those who caused the oppression. They were not content just to patch up the wounds of the poor; they wholeheartedly condemned the causes.

To the prophets such preaching was a vital part of their ministry. They saw it as their life's mission for God to fight for the eradication of injustice. To them any hesitancy in speaking out against such evil meant that faith was lacking. They saw that true faith, and knowledge of God must have both an ethical, and a spiritual content. Although this theme was supremely expressed by the eighth-century prophets; it appears throughout the entire Old Testament, and in the attitudes of Jesus. As J. Miranda has pointed out (*op. cit.*, p. 45), Hosea, when speaking on this theme, intermingled his own expression 'knowledge of Yahweh' (2:22; 5:4; 6:3) with the earlier Israelite tradition 'knowledge of God' (4:1; 6:6). The two expressions were synonymous to Hosea. This would suggest that he knew he was reiterating a theme that had been expressed by others much earlier. On this evidence such a theme can be said to have arisen at least as early as the time when the earliest Old Testament sources were written. The theme therefore takes on a major significance in the overall message of the Old Testament. In the earliest days also God was seen to have at his heart a total compassion for those who were oppressed, and anger against the oppressor. As we shall see, the whole Exodus story is the outworking of this truth.

In Jesus' own teaching we find the same theme present. He denounced the Pharisees and scribes (cf. Matthew 23) in no uncertain terms, declaring that they were so hypocritical that they did not really know God, and 'had neglected the weightier matters of law, justice and mercy and truth'. His attitude to the money changers in the Temple also is a classic response in the manner of the eighth-century prophets themselves. Paul also takes up the theme in his own teaching in Romans. He confirms the idea that God cannot be *known*, when wickedness and injustice are present.

He claims that such wickedness or injustice works against the very truth of God himself. He attacks the 'ungodliness and wickedness (i.e. injustice) of men, who by their wickedness (injustice) suppress the truth' Rom. 1:18. Such a statement reiterated the eighth-century prophets' unequivocal view that God cannot be known at all if injustice, oppression and wickedness are present for they suppress the truth of God himself.

This theme then is of the utmost significance in the Bible. The idea that true knowledge of God involves a total commitment to work for justice, and to identify with the cause of the oppressed and deprived in society, comes out clearly. Justice is not seen as something which God stands for, but rather as an *intrinsic part* of his nature. It is therefore a theme that cannot be taken lightly. It cannot be treated as an isolated idea expressed by one or two prophets from time to time. This idea of what it really means to know God is 'not a tradition *within* the Bible, but rather the biblical tradition itself, the irreducible novelty of the message of the Bible', (Miranda *op. cit.*, p. 53) and must be treated as such by the church of today.

Justice and Worship

In certain parts it becomes clear that not only is it not possible to know God if there is no commitment to fight injustice and stand by those in need, but it is impossible to worship God in truth if that commitment to justice is missing. This idea has been fully expressed by a number of prophets including in particular Amos, Isaiah and Hosea. Each of these prophets was especially critical towards Israel and Judah for their failure to follow God's purpose and plan. They attacked the worship of Israel as being null and void because no account was taken of the injustices that were being perpetrated within their society. They claimed that God considered Israel's worship to be meaningless and hypocritical whilst the people allowed injustice to be practised. Amos prophesies for the Lord saying 'I hate, I despise your feasts, and I take no delight in your solemn assemblies; even though you offer me burnt offerings and cereal offerings, I will not accept them, and the peace offerings of your fatted beasts I will not look upon. Take away from me the noise of your songs; to the melody of your harps I will not listen. But let justice roll down like waters, and righteousness like an overflowing stream' (Amos 5:21–24). Hosea too announces God's demands 'For I desire steadfast love and not sacrifice, the knowledge of God rather than burnt offerings' (Hosea 6:6). And Isaiah is just as critical as Amos of Judah's inadequate attempts to please and worship God,

'Hear the word of the Lord . . . what to me is the multitude of your sacrifices? says the Lord, I have had enough of burnt offerings of rams and the fat of fed beasts; I do not delight in the blood of bulls or of lambs, or of he goats . . . bring no more vain offerings, incense is an abomination to me. New moon and sabbath and the calling of assemblies – I cannot endure iniquity and solemn assembly . . . when you spread forth your hands I will hide my eyes from you; even though you make many prayers, I will not listen, your hands are full of blood. Wash yourselves, make yourselves clean; remove the evil of your doings from before my eyes; cease to do evil, learn to do good; seek justice, correct oppression; defend the fatherless, plead for the widow'. (Isaiah 11:11–17).

The prophets are claiming that God is not to be found in a cultic practice that is unconcerned with evil and unjust living conditions but that he is to be found by seeking out justice and goodness, and by implementing them in society. Miranda claims (*op. cit.*, pp. 53 ff) that the prophets do not just suggest reordering Israel's worship so that the abuses are eliminated, or simply correcting an imbalance between worship and the practical outworking of religion. Rather he suggests that their pleas are much more radical. They claim that only by achieving justice, peace and righteousness will true worship of God ever be achieved. Only by working for complete justice and perfection will God's followers ever be able to worship and adore him. The prophets denounce cultic worship which is an end in itself and which makes God into an idol. Even prayer is criticised by Isaiah, if it is not closely linked to the practical manifestation of justice and the eradication of oppression and greed.

Such criticism of cultic worship, which neglects working for God's justice on earth is not relevant only to the life and times of the eighth-century prophets. This theme occurs throughout the Bible. Jesus' attitude to worship in the teaching of his disciples and his attack on empty outward forms of prayer used by the Pharisees and others, coupled with his practical involvement in healing and in attacking evil wherever it manifested itself, suggests that he was following in the same tradition. Authentic worship was a total offering of the person to the enhancement of God's New Kingdom, just as much for Jesus as for the eighth-century prophets. If we relate this challenging connection between worship and total commitment to the eradication of injustice, to our time we also shall be led to question our worship which is unconcerned with the elimination of the injustices present in our society.

Liberation and Oppression

Although the story of God's direct intervention in world history begins with Abraham, and continues with his inauguration of the Jewish people, his action in liberating the Jewish slaves in Egypt at the Exodus is seen by most Old Testament writers as being the crucial event in the emergence of the Jewish, and consequently Christian, traditions. It was at the Exodus that God most powerfully impressed his will and personality upon the world. It was in the action of the Exodus, that he 'broke into history', revealing his plan and purpose for the world. He did it by choosing a special people for himself, and also by showing his hatred of oppression and injustice. At the Exodus, once and for all, he showed his rejection of oppression, liberated those people who were being deprived of their birthright by others, and then chose those same poor, underprivileged and deprived people to become his chosen race. He declared to the world both his hatred of oppression and injustice and his purpose of restoring the world by means of a weak and abused people.

God reveals this aspect of himself when speaking to Moses. 'Say therefore to the people of Israel "I am the Lord, and (therefore) I will bring you out from under the burdens of the Egyptians, and I will deliver you from their bondage, and I will redeem you with an outstretched arm and with great acts of judgements, and I will take you for my people, and I will be your God; and you shall know that I am the Lord your God, who has brought you out from under the burdens of the Egyptians"'. (Ex. 6:6–7). He is declaring to Moses, to the Jews, and to us, that he is totally opposed to injustice and oppression, and committed to alleviating any misery caused by it. He says 'I am Yahweh . . . and (therefore) I will bring you out . . . deliver you . . . redeem you . . . and I will take you for my people . . . and (then) you shall know that I am Yahweh your God.' Because he is God, he is opposed to injustice. Because he is God, he will free the oppressed. And it is in the liberation of the poor and oppressed that he will actually be recognised as God.

It was this view of God then, that became deeply embedded in the faith of the Israelites. Their God was the one who had acted to free them from oppression. 'A wandering Aramean was my father; and he went down into Egypt and sojourned there, And the Egyptians treated us harshly, and afflicted us and laid upon us hard bondage. Then we cried to the Lord the God of our fathers, and the Lord heard our voice, and saw our affliction, our toil, and our oppression; and the Lord brought us up out of Egypt with a mighty hand . . .' (Deut. 26:5–8). God was seen by generation after generation as someone who heard the cries of those who were oppressed, and came to rescue them.

The same view of God's righteousness and committment to justice, is expressed much later by Jeremiah. He prophesies for God saying that 'anyone who knows me knows ... that I am the Lord who practises kindness, justice and righteousness in the earth' (Jer. 9:24). And Ezekiel agrees when he prophesies 'And they shall know that I am the Lord when I break the bars of their yoke, and deliver them from the land of those who enslaved them' (Ch. 34:27). They both have the same view of God, as the one who expresses himself to the world through the liberation of those who cry for help. Although God delivered the people of Israel from slavery when they cried to him, later they suffered at God's hand, because his committment to the Jews was dependent on their commitment to his justice. When Israel began to veer away from God's purposes, rather than following his ways of justice, and began to oppress others they incurred God's wrath: God's prophets began to curse them because, rather than making the most of God's liberation, they took away the liberty of others. When they refused to heed God's word, both Northern and Southern kingdoms were defeated and sent into exile.

Amos was the prophet who put God's principles to the Northern kingdom. He castigated them saying 'Woe to those who live upon beds of ivory, and stretch themselves upon their couches, and eat lambs from the flock, and calves from the midst of the stall. . . . Therefore shall they now be the first of those to go into exile, and the revelry of those who stretch themselves shall pass away' (Ch. 6:4, 7). Because they took no notice of him, the kingdom did pass away within a few years, to the Assyrians. Later on in the Southern kingdom the same thing happened. Isaiah, Micah and Jeremiah, all spoke out, yet they were not heeded. Jeremiah puts the point clearly, when he offers the people a last chance. 'If you truly execute justice, one with another, if you do not oppress the alien, the fatherless, or the widow ... and if you do not go after other gods to your own hurt, then I will let you dwell in this place, in the land that I gave of old to your fathers for ever' (Ch. 7:5–7). But they do not take the offer; they refuse to turn from the twin evils that God hates, injustice and idolatry, and so God finally allows Jerusalem to fall into the hands of the Babylonians.

The idea of liberation for those who are oppressed takes yet another turn. Later during the exile when the Israelites were once more being persecuted and oppressed, Ezekiel raises again the theme of the Exodus. He speaks to the people in exile, saying that if they are truly repentant and call upon their God in their time of need, he will hear them and release them just as he did in Egypt. And as Zimmerli points out (*Gesammelte Aufsatze*, pp. 43–4) Ezekiel continually expresses the same idea as in Ex. 6:6–7 'You shall know me when I do such and such a thing . . .' – as in the already quoted passage 'They shall know that I am the Lord when I break the bars of their yoke, and deliver them from the land of those who enslave them' (Ez. 34:27). So the theme of liberation is used once more. Israel will be set free so long as she returns to God's ways of justice and righteousness.

Economic exploitation and the suffering incurred, caused God to act to save the people of Israel at the Exodus and to lead them to a new land, and a new pupose. Later, economic exploitation by the Jews led him to disassociate himself from them, because they rejected his purpose and plan. Then, when Israel had suffered sufficient punishment and was being exploited by another oppressor, God liberated those Jews who were truly repentant. The theme of justice expounded by the prophets stems from the idea of liberation from oppression as expressed by God at the Exodus. A commitment to stand beside and help those who are being deprived, exploited, and oppressed, whether openly, or subtly, can therefore be seen as intrinsic to the nature of God himself and essential to anybody who would be his follower, for to accept God's perfect nature is to commit oneself to fight and eliminate the evil created by selfishness and greed.

Love

This particular theme of God's commitment to justice on earth continues into the New Testament. Miranda (*op. cit.*, p. 63) very helpfully links Jesus' second commandment to its original context in Leviticus. This commandment, that we should love our neighbour as ourselves is a quotation from Leviticus 19:18. In its context there, it is the positive culmination of a whole series of 'do nots'. The people of Israel were not to steal, deal falsely, lie, rob their neighbour, oppress the deaf or blind, be partial in judgement to rich or poor, slander or hate their neighbour, but rather they were to love their neighbour as themselves (cf. Lev. 19:11–18). This call to love comes after a 'series of prohibitions which all concern the most rigorous justice' (Miranda *op. cit.*, p. 63). Love therefore, to Jesus, was the culmination of the idea of working for justice within society. In speaking of love Jesus was speaking in the tradition of the prophets.

Love in the New Testament is not therefore, a new concept at all but rather the continuing of the earlier theme of justice. Love means working towards God's plan for the world. It means commitment to eliminating all injustice, oppression and deprivation. Love in this sense is very practical. It is not just a theoretical concept that affects thoughts and words alone; it involves actions as well. Love cannot be expressed only in 'spiritual' concerns. Being so closely connected to justice it must of necessity be expressed in concern for every aspect of man.

But love is seen to be intimately connected not only with the theme of justice from the Old Testament: we find that it is also closely related to the Old Testament view of knowing God. Just as Jeremiah talked of Josiah's knowledge of God saying 'He judged the cause of the poor and needy . . . is not this to know me?" says the Lord' (Ch. 22:16), so John describes knowledge of God in terms of love, which we have already seen is intimately connected to justice. 'Beloved, let us love one another; for love is of God, and he who loves is born of God and knows God. He who does not love does not know God; for God is love' (1 John 4:7–8). For John to know God is to love one another. John develops what he means by this kind of love, this true knowledge of God. He gives this example as well as many others! 'If any one has the world's goods and sees his brother in need, yet closes his heart against him, how does God's love abide in him? Little children, let us not love in word or speech but in deed and in truth' (1 John 3:17–18. James 2:15 ff). An intrinsic part of knowing God is loving, and fighting for the cause of, our neighbour. He states clearly, that there cannot be the first without the second, that knowing and loving, loving and being committed to serving the needs of the underprivileged, are all part of the one whole experience of man coming into touch with God. He also talks about it in very practical terms. When he talks of a man who has the world's goods and a brother who is in need, he is talking about wealth and poverty similar to that which we experience today. He is talking about the gap between the industrial west and the Third World. He is talking about good living conditions, and good educational facilities, as compared to high rise, high density, cheaply built modern inner city estates. These are the issues where the practical outworking of his words must be found today. The New Testament takes up the themes of love, justice, knowledge and liberation of the poor, expressed so decisively in the Old Testament. It confirms for us how such themes are central not only to the Jewish tradition, but also to the Christian tradition as well. We shall now move on to look particularly at the life and death of Christ. How does the incarnation theme confirm God's special identification with those who are in need, who are deprived, and who seek justice, as we have seen in the Old Testament? Does it go further, to express an even deeper concern, and special commitment to the needy through the life and teaching of Jesus Christ?

Incarnation

The Old Testament has given us a description of God that certainly is not lacking in majesty. On reading it, we become immediately aware of God's greatness and man's position before him. One would have expected that same aura of majesty to have surrounded his Son not only in his birth but also his whole life on earth. However, as we turn to the New Testament, we find a paradox. The Son, who was worthy of the highest possible welcome that man could offer, receives the opposite, and this was not due just to man's neglect; rather God chose that his Son, from his birth to his death, should identify not with the greatest that the world could offer, but with the least. Take for example Jesus' birth. It was beset by a host of problems and difficulties for Mary and Joseph right from the start. To begin with, they were forced to make a long, arduous donkey journey, just a few days before Jesus was due to be born. That meant that Mary was deprived of all the normal help and security, that a mother to be would expect at home. After being turned from every door, the only shelter was a stable.

Not only were there physical hardships to be endured; Jesus was born out of wedlock; he was born into a subject race. The Jewish people of the time were not autonomous, but were controlled by the Roman powers and some puppet Jewish despots. Although Joseph had a job the family was far from wealthy.

As soon as Jesus was born he was hated, and rejection was to follow him throughout his life. The powerful Herod was so frightened of him that he had all the male babies in the area killed. Imagine the feelings of Mary and Joseph as they ran for their baby's life, all the way down to Egypt. From the start Jesus experienced not just deprivation, but also hate, fear, and homelessness. And when the family did return to Nazareth, they must have been thought different.

Jesus could perhaps have forgotten his humble origins but rather than attempting to forget his background and climb the ladder to a better social position he dedicated his life to serving that very same part of society from which he had come. From the beginning of his ministry he declared this aim, and continued it throughout his life to his death. When asked to lead worship at the synagogue in

Nazareth, his home town he read from Isaiah: 'The Spirit of the Lord is upon me because he has anointed me to preach good news to the poor. He has sent me to proclaim release to the captives and recovery of sight to the blind, to set at liberty those who are oppressed, to proclaim the acceptable year of the Lord' (Luke 4:18–19).

By reading such a passage, Jesus was restating the task of the Messiah and identifying himself with that task. A major part of his ministry would be to continue to express God's love, concern and commitment to the deprived of the world. By relating his own ministry to the words of Isaiah, he was showing that he was going to continue the liberation of the oppressed that started when God freed the Jewish slaves in Egypt, continued when he expressed through Amos, Micah and Hosea his concern for those who were still oppressed, and ended with his restoration of the Jews of the exile. Jesus was identifying himself with this aspect of God: He knew that part of the nature of the 'Good News' itself, was that its foremost appeal would be to those who were being deprived of part, or all, of their humanity. He knew that one of the chief purposes of the Kingdom was to alleviate the suffering of the poor and to bring them justice. In the beatitudes he said that the poor were blessed (Mt. 5:3). Were they not blessed because the Kingdom had arrived bringing with it a commitment to eradicate the poverty and suffering they were experiencing? (cf. *Good News to the Poor* – Julio de S. Ana, pp. 16–17) Jesus was not trying to glorify the plight of the needy, but telling them that the coming of the Kingdom would bring an end to their suffering. Such passages show no divorce between the material and the spiritual. The Good News of the Kingdom of God is, that in a practical way it will liberate the poor.

Jesus lived his commitment to the poor. He had none of the benefits during his ministry of the comfortable security of a job, a home, a family and a regular income. He gave himself instead to a life of insecurity so that he could serve the needs of others. He shared men's sufferings and often healed them, and told richer people why they, in their own way, were suffering (though often this advice went unheeded and the rich and powerful usually felt very antagonistic towards him). In his teaching in Mt. 25:31–46 Jesus made it clear that he *was* the poor: 'Truly, I say to you, as you did it not to one of the least of these, you did it not to me' v 45). And we neglect seeing Christ in everyone in need at our peril. He expected his followers to find themselves "in the poor" just as much as he did (cf. *The Two Alienated Faces of the One Church* – Benoit Dumas and Bonino's reference to it: 'The Struggle for the

Poor and the Church' in *The Ecumenical Review*, Vol. 28, No. 1, pp. 40–41).

It is interesting to study Jesus' message to John the Baptist in prison. When John sent a message to Jesus asking if he really was the Messiah, Jesus did not answer directly – 'Yes'. Instead he told John's messenger, 'Go and see for yourself, and then report that back to John.' Jesus knew that his practical ministry was the fulfilment of Isaiah's words; that the inauguration of his New Kingdom involved a very practical expression of a new vision and experience of life. He knew that John's messenger had only to witness his healing and preaching to be convinced of the answer to Johns' question.

Jesus realised, however, that he could not serve the needs of the poor by helping them just as individuals. He attacked the greed and wealth of the powerful oppressor, as much as he satisfied the practical needs of those oppressed.

We have already noted Jesus' attack on the extortionate money changers and grasping traders in the Court of the Temple. He castigated also the powerful religious leaders who used their status for their own personal satisfaction and took scant interest in the rest of the population to whom they could well have been of service. In the beatitudes, not only did he bless the poor and hungry but he also, a few verses later, chastises and curses the rich and greedy for their selfishness (Luke 6:20–26).

Jesus' teaching on the misuse of wealth and power, and blindness to suffering, has a special relevance to the wealthy in every society, particularly if they happen to be religious people, hoping to be accepted into God's presence. In the parable of the sheep and goats Jesus talks of the Son of Man sitting in judgement. The sheep are those whose knowledge of God led them to serve those in need, poverty, distress and suffering around them, whereas the goats are those who did not really know God at all, because they did not respond to the needs of those all around them who were crying for help. This parable reminds us of the Old Testament teaching about the knowledge of God involving a commitment to fight for the oppressed. This teaching is a warning to the rich and wealthy within the church down the ages, who consider that they know God personally through their faith and yet who are completely oblivious of the comparative poverty existing on the other side of town, and the absolute poverty shown everyday on the TV news. What Jesus began in a stable, and continued in his associations with the outcasts and more lowly members of Jewish society, he finally fulfilled in his way of dying. His arrest, trial and death, reflect as clearly as every other part of his life his commitment to those unjustly treated by society. In fact it is in Christ's death that we see his absolute, and total commitment to the oppressed and powerless. Not only was he prepared to be unpopular, scorned and derided for his message, but he was also prepared to die for it; this was the extent of his commitment to those who are unjustly treated. To be crucified with a convicted murderer, to die with outcasts outside the city wall, to be mocked and scourged with no one to stand up for him, to be forsaken by all his friends, to be condemned on evidence that even the judges knew and admitted was totally inadequate, to be used as a pawn by a governor to appease mob demands; all of these things Jesus experienced as a man showing to the whole world that the Christ was fully prepared to suffer and die rather than turn and appeal to the wealthy and powerful in order to live.

Not only did Christ identify himself with the oppressed in his death, but he challenged his followers to do the same in their own lives. As J. Bonino puts it so clearly (*Revolution Theology Come of Age*, p. 145) 'At the same time, we are called to this same identity in the double identification with the crucified Christ; and therefore with those with whom he himself was identified, the outcast, the oppressed, the poor, the forsaken, the sinners, the lost. This is the cradle of the Christian's identity and relevance. To be crucified together with Christ means to stand with those for whose sake God Himself died the death of the sacrilege, the subversive, the God forsaken one.' The cross therefore stands before us to prove that Jesus' identification with the powerless and poor, rather than with the powerful and wealthy, was not just a mistake in God's plan for incarnation, not a message of words without actions, but that it was an identification that was carried out from the start to the finish of Christ's life on earth.

Paternalism and Human Rights

It may seem as though Jesus favoured the poor. Does this mean that God views people unequally, that the poor are more important to him than the rich? Are the rich 'second class citizens' in God's eyes? Not at all; this would be a distortion of God's message. God has no favourites. The God of the Bible looks upon the rich and the poor, as people, and therefore of equal value in his sight. The passage in Leviticus 19:15 already quoted, confirms this. 'You shall do no injustice in judgement; you shall not be partial to the poor or defer to the great, but in righteousness shall you judge your neighbour'. God is impartial, but there is a reason why he still has a *bias* towards the poor and oppressed.

In God's original purpose and creation, he made sufficient resources in the world for every created human being to have a reasonable share, even allowing for the diversity of gifts within different individuals. After the fall, some humans became greedy and took more than their share, denying others what is rightfully theirs. God's concern therefore, at the very start of his relationship with fallen man, is to demand that the balance be redressed. He is committed to those who have been denied their birthright, and men will be completely equal before God's judgement only when they treat each other equally.

Serving the poor therefore, to God, to Jesus and to the Christian is not a matter of paternalism, of alleviating suffering and distress. It is giving back to the poor what is rightfully theirs; recognising the rights that the poor person has because he is a created being; and it is a seeking of ways to restore those rights to him. This is the difference between paternalism and true Christian love. For the Christian God is not interested in paternalistic giving, he is interested only in every person's receiving what is his rightful God-given inheritance. As Bigo puts it – 'The supreme delicacy of Charity (Christian love) is to recognise the right of the person being given to' (*Doctrine Sociale*, p. 378). Far from favouring the poor at the expense of the rich, God and his Son are seeking to redress the imbalance developed ever since the Fall.

If we look at the ministry of Jesus for our example we find he is quite happy to talk to both rich and poor, happy to accept the friendship of either, regardless of their position. Nevertheless, when he talks to them, his message to the rich is different from that to the poor. To both of them he says 'Come follow me' – but he had to remind the rich young ruler that if he wished to follow him he had to be prepared to give up the wealth that was his so that the poor could receive their rightful share. Jesus makes it clear that nothing can be more important to a follower than his love for God – not even wealth. The rich and powerful must be prepared to give up their position of power, if they want to follow God (i.e. the God who loves all who are denied their true humanity by the present powerful and greedy people within the world). Jesus was not joking when he said that it was easier for a camel to go through the eye of a needle than for a rich man to enter the Kingdom of God. He knew how difficult it would be for a man, who is using something that belongs to someone else, to turn and give back what is not his. But that is what his creator demands of him, as a pre-requisite to any real relationship.

CHAPTER FIVE

Biblical Attitudes Towards Ownership and Possessions

Having looked in the previous chapter at the way God has viewed the poor and oppressed within the world, and the ways in which he has sought to identify himself with them we now turn to consider some more practical matters that have a direct bearing on the presence of poverty and oppression in society, and what the biblical response is to them. For just as we have seen God's word has been directed towards the politics of men, societies, and world structures, we will find that God is also intimately concerned with the economics of his created order. Economic relationships between people from a biblical point of view are just as subject to God's will and purpose as every other aspect of life. God is as concerned for the economic needs of man, and for the just economic development of the universe, as he is for every other sphere of man's existence.

In this chapter we shall be looking at a few distinctive economic issues that deeply affect the lives of every person in our society. We must necessarily start with the subject of ownership. This is a subject that already vexes world politicians and is the foundation stone of the three key economic philosophies of our day; capitalism, socialism and communism. We must therefore see whether the Bible has anything distinctive to say in the contemporary debate about ownership.

Ownership

British society has an equivocal attitude towards ownership. Our understanding is influenced partly by the capitalist emphasis on private ownership, individual free enterprise, profit and competition. It is also influenced by the socialist emphasis on the corporate responsibilities of a nation, on Government control, on the redistribution of wealth through taxation, and on the public ownership of some sections of industry, commerce and the economic infrastructure that closely effects the lives of everyone.

Ownership, no matter by whom, is absolute, is upheld by law, and is crucial to the system. If a man owns something, it is his by right and it cannot be legally taken away from him without fair restitution. Ownership relates to land, capital, property and every other aspect of life. It gives the owner the right to any profit, income or interest gained from the original possession. And once ownership has been proven in law, the method of acquisition is not usually queried. Ownership is inviolate.

However, when we come to look at the biblical attitude towards ownership, we find that a very different view emerges. We find that God does not seem to grant absolute ownership of property, wealth or land, to man at all.

It would appear that from both the Old and New Testaments that God is not opposed in principle to private ownership.* The difference between God's views and society's views is not related to the issue of public or private ownership. It lies in what is actually meant by 'ownership' and what the rights are that are bestowed on the owner. For whereas our society grants absolute rights to the owner of property, the Bible sets out the principles of ownership of property and land by man in far more qualified terms.

Let us look first at *land*. To the Israelites after the entry into Canaan, land was the most important form of wealth. In those days it was as much the source of wealth as capital is today. A great deal of the early writings and the laws are intimately concerned with land, its ownership, its use, its sale, its inheritance, and the responsibilities that went with it.

It is quite clear that land, i.e. the ultimate source of all wealth and power in Old Testament society, is owned by God, and by God alone. It does not belong to mankind. Psalm 24:1 states 'The earth is the Lord's and the fullness thereof, the world and those who dwell therein'. The same idea is worked out in detail in Leviticus 25 where God explains to the Israelites about the land and their use of it. He starts from the same basic standpoint. 'When you come into the land which I shall give you' (v 2). The land is first seen to be given by God. Then as we read on in the chapter we find that God is not giving the land to the people absolutely, but that there are

* See note on p. 95

a whole list of commands concerning its use. This suggests that man, rather than being given absolute ownership of the land, is being given only its stewardship. The idea of jubilee in this chapter encourages this principle. For God distributes the land, to start with, to his trustees. Then every 49 years, at the jubilee, it is to go back to God's original trustees. This pattern stresses that no man owns the land and so it cannot be bought or sold outright. 'The land shall not be sold in perpetuity, for the land is mine; for you are strangers and sojourners with me (Lev. 25:23).'

So God implants in Israel the concept of their being trustees and stewards of land and wealth that can really be truly owned only by God himself. It is assumed that, as God created the world, it is his by right, and that any rights granted to humanity concerning ownership and land are only derived from God, and are not intrinsically human. Creation and ownership go together; human ownership of land and wealth is derived from the ownership of God.

The essential difference between ownership and stewardship is that stewardship shows man's dependence on God for his existence and for his abilities and possessions (cf. article by Chris Wright in *Third Way*, Issues 9–11). He is therefore a steward or trustee, rather than an owner, in his relationship both with God and with other men.

The creation ordinance which gives man dominion over nature (Genesis) is not a case of ownership being handed over outright to man. As C. Wright points out (*op. cit.*) even if man is given the overall responsibility of looking after nature, it is only in the sense that he has a 'common ownership' of the world's resources, which are to be for the benefit of the *whole* of mankind. It is not that man is given the gift of 'private and absolute ownership' of small parts of nature for his own private use. The gift of God's world to man is never seen as an absolute gift in the Bible, nor is it a gift to the individual. It is something bestowed, unearned, on mankind as a family.

Although God grants stewardship to man, he will not tolerate any attempt to usurp his position as absolute owner. When man tries to play at God, or when a steward tries to assume ownership, God will be forced to deny that man completely, because although man has the ability to do what he wants with power and wealth in his lifetime, it is only a transient, provisional power. Whereas our society claims that a man's ownership of property and wealth is absolute, the Bible is committed to the view that for man, nothing is absolutely his; all that he has is given to him as a trustee/steward by his Creator/Father God.

Consumption

Just as society today accepts outright ownership of property and wealth, so too it accepts the right of the owner to do whatever he wants with the proceeds from such wealth. Whatever income a man receives from the working of his wealth, he is entitled to use as he wishes. He does not have to be involved in the production process of the firm in which the capital is invested. The only restriction imposed upon an owner of wealth is that he must pay tax on the income he receives to pay for goods and services provided by society. And the scale is such that the more someone earns from their property and capital, the higher the tax rate will be. In a small way society has demanded that its richer members should make reparation to the poorer members through the tax system. However, proposals are being made to reduce this kind of tax burden upon the owners of wealth, for it is said to be unfair. In other words such taxation is not seen to be morally right, but just the policy of an earlier government administration that was more socialist than capitalist.

The biblical understanding of the role of man as a steward or trustee has a particular bearing on the matter of consumption. For although the steward is called to use his gifts and abilities to the fullest to achieve the greatest overall production, he is not necessarily entitled to consume it all. If he does so he will destroy the balance between the population and the resources available. Only by allowing the total production to be fairly shared out will men be proper stewards of God's creation.

If we bear in mind the steward's role, to produce in order to satisfy the needs of mankind and develop the world in the process, what view shall we have concerning consumption of produce? The attitude running right through the Bible is that consumption ought to be determined far more according to *needs*, than according to the ability to produce (cf. *A Christian Critique of Capitalism* – D. Hay, p. 17). 'From each according to his ability – to each according to his needs' seems to be a phrase, though not from the Bible that expresses the very heart of biblical thought. As we shall see later, it is a principle that lay right at the centre of the early New Testament church. It is only through such a view of consumption and stewardship that God's creation and mankind as a race have a hope of survival.

Not only does stewardship of material possessions bring productivity and development, it also brings *responsibility*. The early Old Testament writings, concerned with how the new race in the Promised Land was to live its life and grow worthily as God's people, had a great deal to say about the reponsibilities of belonging to God. To be a member of God's family, to be given abilities, land and God's protection, brought also the responsibility of behaving and living as God wanted you to live. This meant caring for your neighbour, your family, the old people and children, the sick or handicapped, the people in the community who were less adequate, or who had lesser abilities or little wealth. It meant contributing to the overall needs of the community, sharing out the benefits of production amongst the whole of society and not limiting it to the producers or capital owners. The message now has equal relevance to a world that is in danger of collapse because consumption of production no longer accords to patterns of responsible biblical stewardship.

Unlimited Liability

The early church took very seriously the matter of stewardship which was central to their whole response to the Christian message after the coming of the Holy Spirit at Pentecost. We must take it equally seriously today, if we are in any way concerned about responding to Christ's call to follow him in the twentieth century.

During his own three-year ministry with his disciples, Jesus set the example that later developed more fully. He, of course, had very few possessions, and owned nothing of high material value. But the group did appear to have some money, which was kept in a common purse. The group shared not only their friendships, their journeys, their experiences, and their way of life together, they also shared their financial resources. Rather than being outside the disciples' closely-knit relationship with Jesus, finance was an integral part of their lives together. Indeed from time to time Jesus had quite a lot to say about money and possessions and man's dependence on them; his teaching was part of a new way of living.

This sharing of financial resources was automatically continued with the emergence of the new church after Pentecost. It developed even further involving not only money but other possessions, including land and property. When the activities of the early church are summed up (Acts 2:43–47, 4:32–37) there are direct references to the integral nature of economic sharing within the church; they had all things in common – so that everyone's needs were satisfied. Examples are given where members with land and capital sold these to satisfy the needs of others in the church. One person's surplus was made available to satisfy another person's needs.

However, it does need to be recognised that this was not a compulsory practice within the church. It was not demanded of church members that they should give up their private property automatically. The story of Ananias and Sapphira (Ch. 5:1–11) records that there was no compulsion on anyone to sell what they had. Peter fully accepts that while the property was his, Ananias had every right to do what he liked with it. The sin that led to Ananias' death was the fact that he lied about the sum he made on the property, and the sum he put into the community fund. It would seem therefore that it was a regular practice in the early church that when there was need, those who had property and possessions might well sell them in order to satisfy the need. The tense of the verb in Acts 2:45 and 4:34 supports this (*Rich Christians in an Age of Hunger*, R. Sider, p. 100). The imperfect tense is used, which suggests a continuing process rather than a once-and-for-all act; i.e. 'they were in the habit of regularly bringing the proceeds of what was being sold'.

This principle of church members sharing their wealth with those who were in need (cf. *Rich Christians in an Age of Hunger* – Sider, and *Good News to the Poor* – Santa Ana) is central to the life and teaching of the church in the time of Paul as well. Paul illustrates the point in both a negative and positive way in his letters to the Corinthian Church. In his first letter (Ch. 11:20–22) he roundly condemns the practice, at the Eucharist and Agape, of the rich bringing their own food and eating it themselves, side by side with poorer members who could not afford to take any food at all and went hungry. He assumed that at such a 'coming together' those who had more than necessary would surely share with those in need. In his second letter, he puts the point even more strongly (Ch. 8:13–15). When talking about giving financial support to other Christians in need, he says 'I do not mean that others should be eased and you burdened, but that as a matter of equality your abundance at the present time should supply their want so that their abundance may supply your want, that there may be equality.' Paul considers it right for Christians to share out their surpluses to areas of need, whenever the matter arises. This will mean that support may flow one way at one time, and another way at another time, so encouraging equality. No doubt he saw such sharing in other than financial terms. (After all it was the Jerusalem church who originally 'shared' the Gospel with the Corinthians – so now the offer of financial assistance was just 'balancing the account' in a very practical manner.)

Paul goes on to emphasise the principle by turning to the Old Testament. He quotes the story of Moses and the Israelites in the desert, when they picked up the manna for food. 'He who gathered much had nothing over, and he who gathered little had no lack' (Ex. 16:18). Paul, by returning to the heart of the biblical view of ownership, is calling Christians to view everything they have as a gift from the God who owns all and provides faithfully. He is calling them therefore to surrender their right to any surplus of possessions, and to share liberally with those who need.

So a principle of ownership clearly emerges from the early church practices that continues Old Testament traditions. It does not deny the right to private ownership, but it endorses the idea of stewardship, and encourages the sharing of one person's surplus to meet another person's need. As R. Sider has succinctly put it – 'Oneness in Christ for the earliest Christian community meant unlimited economic liability for, and total economic availability to, the other members of Christ's body' (*op. cit.* p. 101). Unlimited economic liability between members of the church is a very challenging thought for today, the more so because it is an expression of a principle of ownership that God has revealed clearly and unmistakably, right through the Old and New Testaments. It cannot therefore be written off as a particular contemporary attitude of the early Jerusalem church, which led to its economic ruin and later need for support from Macedonia.*

The Christian attitude towards ownership and sharing, fulfils God's gradual revelation of his attitude towards material possessions, throughout the Bible. Just as Jesus fulfils the message of the Old Testament, so too the early church's attitude towards economic sharing fulfils the Old Testament view of ownership and stewardship, whereby the wealthy share their wealth with those in need (cf. *The Jubilee Ordinances*).

Paul shows that this sharing took place also between the churches. Examples are the collection in the Antioch churches for the famine-starved church at Jerusalem (Acts 11) and the major collection undertaken by Paul throughout Asia Minor, which he took back to the Jerusalem church himself. Such inter-church sharing illustrates the very great awareness that Paul knew Christians ought to have of one another's practical and economic needs. This awareness was not an 'added extra' to the Christian life. For Paul, it lay at the very heart of the Christian message itself. As he says, when

---

* This failure to be self-supporting was due to the very heavy financial strain that the Jerusalem Church was under at this time because of the great number of poor and beggars who came to the City to beg from the pilgrims, and then became dependent on the Jerusalem Church; there was also a serious famine in Palestine between AD 44 and 48 (cf. Josephus and Acts 11:27–30; both of which factors must have combined to drain the church's resources).

encouraging the Macedonians to give to the collection, giving should be automatic because of Christ's supreme example: 'For you know the grace of our Lord Jesus Christ, that though he was rich, yet for your sake he became poor, so that by his poverty you might become rich.' (2 Cor. 8:9.)'

Extremes

The next distinctive economic issue that we shall consider is one that affects everyone today, yet it is often accepted without question – namely extremes of wealth and poverty. The Pentateuch writers all assume and accept the overall ownership by God of all land, and hence, all wealth. The bestowal of land by God upon the Israelites is seen as a gift to them, a symbol of their covenant relationship. That relationship they see as one that grants them their freedom and yet at the same time demands their wholehearted response to and acknowledgement of God. If the land is seen as God's gift to them, they see their response as obeying God's laws set out in the Pentateuch. Their use of land and wealth was subject to instructions laid down by God.

They also assumed that God, when he originally distributed the land to the people of Israel, distributed it in a fair way, dividing it fairly between each tribe, each clan and each family, enabling every family to make a living, and to have sufficient to be economically independent even though they were part of a larger economic whole.

Given these two assumptions, we can see just what God sought to convey to his people, with regard to economic and social equality. God saw the economic structure of his people as a crucial factor in their overall social development. He was particualry concerned that, as the community grew, the rights of every member would be protected, for God puts a higher value on man than on any other commodity – even land or wealth. As W. Eichrodt has put it 'The life of even the most degraded person is worth more than the richest possession' ('The Question of Property in the light of the Old Testament' in *Biblical Authority for Today*, ed. A. Richardson & W. Schweitzer). Knowing that the unchecked growth of wealth and poverty leads to the devaluation of human life, God set up a series of mechanisms that, if carried out, would have ensured that poverty and wealth never really developed to any great extent. Behind them is the idea that any poverty that developed in the community had to be stopped by redistribution of surplus.

All these mechanisms were set up to develop a social structure suited to the time and place, to produce a 'social fabric of multiple household land – tenure, and the comparative equality and independence of family – plus – land units' (C. Wright – 'Ethics and the Old Testament – the Jubilee' in *Third Way*). Such a fabric would give freedom to each individual and family in Israel, and yet at the same time, allow Israel to develop and grow as a community and nation under God, while preventing an accumulation of wealth in the hands of a few powerful families in each tribe, or its passing on from generation to generation, without any chance of the stranglehold being broken. Indeed it provided ways in which, from time to time, debts could be cancelled and landlessness could be overridden, giving the family a chance to have a fresh start and escape the vicious circle of deep-seated poverty. Such structures were set up to 'protect the human rights of those who regularly fell behind the more aggressive and successful members of society' (C. Wright *op. cit.*).

These safeguards come in Leviticus 25, Deuteromony 15 and Exodus 23, and concern the institutions of the Jubilee, Redemption, the Sabbatical Year and various smaller laws set up to help the poor in Jewish society. As I have stated earlier, there seems little evidence that the Jubilee or the Sabbatical Year were actually kept by Israel; apparently even they were not keen on the principles involved. Yet God's revelation of them in the Law still stands; they are still principles that are intrinsic to God's plan and purpose, regardless of whether man takes any notice of them or not, and if one looks at the prophetic utterances around the time when both the Northern and Southern Kingdoms were defeated, and taken into exile, the defeat and the collapse of their societies could be attributed to their neglect of the principles involved in the Jubilee and Sabbatical Year. They had turned from being the oppressed into being the oppressors.

The principle of the Jubilee (Lev. 25) was that every 50 years all property should be returned to the original owners, to give fresh opportunities to those who had 'lost out' for one reason or another and encourage every household to be independent, rather than servile and reduce the possibility of a person being penalised by the poverty or servitude of his parents, or grandparents (which might have been caused by no fault of theirs – e.g. the death of a breadwinner in the family). It would not cripple the wealthy, but would show them that all the wealth they possessed was not theirs – but God's.

The Jubilee was to be backed up by the system or redemption (Lev. 25:25–55). This involved the looking after and support of a poor member by others in his clan. If someone got into debt for some reason or other, he was to be looked after by other members of the clan. They were to lend him money interest free, or mortgage his land and possessions, so that he could still live and trade. And if the poor person still could not survive, the clansman had to make him a slave treating him, however, only as an ordinary workman. Such a system of economic redemption, meant that the distribution of the land would normally remain in its original clan, or tribe, but that within the clan, there would be some families who would become far wealthier than others. But the Jubilee principle was to ensure that this was not to go on for too long. After two generations the wealth and land, the debts and slaves, were all to be released and returned to their original family, so that a fresh start could be made. This would ensure the continued existence of the small independent family unit with their land, each directly aware of God's covenant to them personally (cf. C. Wright) through what he had given to them. The wealthy would then never get too wealthy and the poor would never get so poor that they could not break out of the vicious circle of poverty.

Another law designed to combat greed and exploitation was the Sabbatical Year. This was not just a good agricultural idea of leaving the land fallow from time to time, as in modern crop rotation systems. It had a far wider significance. True it started with the land, (Ex. 23:10-11, Lev. 25:1-7), but it concerned also the releasing of debts (Deut. 15:1-2) and the freeing of slaves (Deut. 15:12-18). The intention of the law was made quite plain. The fallow year on the land was so that the poor could reap and glean anything that grew on the land that year (Ex. 23:11), incidentally benefiting the soil. The releasing of debtors by their creditors (Deut. 15:1-6) was so that everyone would remember that even the prosperity of the rich is dependent on God's bounty, and that there was a time when every person was a slave in Egypt. The message was further endorsed by the command that the slave owner should give the slave a bonus from his herds when he was freed, to prevent him from slipping straight back into debt and slavery.

So the Sabbatical Year ordinances had a real purpose in aiming to improve the position of those in extreme poverty. God called all his people to work to reduce such poverty 'For the poor will never cease out of the land; therefore I command you. You shall open wide your land to your brother, to the needy and to the poor in the land' (Deut. 15:11). Other ordinances encourage the same openhanded justice. The principle of tithing (Deut. 14:28-29), as well as being a tax to help the Levites, was to be given also to the fatherless and the widows who made up quite a percentage of the poor in the society of that day. The principle of gleaning, that we remember from the story of Ruth, reminds us of the rights given to the poor to pick up the grain left on a farmer's land, and to reap the corners of the fields. Many of God's laws were designed to safeguard the rights of the poor and ensure a just society, by commanding his people *not* to allow extremes of poverty and wealth, but *rather* to work to eliminate such extremes.

However, such practical laws concerning Jubilee, Sabbatical Years, and gleaning seem scarcely relevant to the modern world Christians face today. It would be impossible to implement laws made for a primitive agricultural existence in our modern technological age. But the underlying principle has every possible significance in today's world.

Materialism

[handwritten note: We create so many idols.]

Jesus was continually pointing out that to attach too much importance to things and objects that are derived and therefore secondary, instead of worshipping the one from whom all things are derived, is idolatrous. The rich farmer, who builds bigger barns and then never lives to see them full (Luke 12:16–21) was ridiculed by Jesus. And the beatitudes make this point time and again. In Matthew we read how vital it is not to value this world's possessions more highly than God himself; 'Do not be anxious about your life, what you shall eat, nor about your body, what you shall put on. For life is more than food, and the body more than clothing. Consider the ravens: they neither sow nor reap, they have neither storehouse nor barn, and yet God feeds them. Of how much more value are you than the birds! And which of you by being anxious can add a cubit to his span of life? If then you are not able to do as small a thing as that, why are you anxious about the rest? Consider the lilies, how they grow; they neither toil nor spin; yet I tell you, even Solomon in all his glory was not arrayed like one of these. But if God so clothes the grass which is alive in the field today and tomorrow is thrown into the oven, how much more will he clothe you, O men of little faith! And do not seek what you are to to eat and what you are to drink, nor be of anxious mind. For all the nations of the world seek these things; and your Father knows that you need them. Instead, seek his kingdom, and these things shall be yours as well' (Mt. 6:25–33).

Of course it is not that such material possessions are innately evil, and that they automatically pervert man. Nowhere in the Bible is there such a negative view of the creation. It is man who perverts his relationship with creation by setting it higher than its Creator. This is what cuts man off from God. Paul warns Timothy: 'But those who desire to be rich fall into temptation, into a snare, into many senseless and hurtful desires that plunge men into ruin and destruction. For the *love* of money is the root of all evils; it is through this craving that some have wondered away from the faith (1 Tim. 6:9–10).

Modern man has fallen into idolatry, as much as the Jews did in Old Testament times. Material things are now worshipped in place of God, contrary to everything that Jesus and his followers preached. Indeed, the prophecy of Isaiah, referring to idols cut out of cedar trees, applies just as much in today's materialistic world, where possessions do not give the satisfaction and ultimate peace of mind that is demanded of them any more than did the cedar-tree idols. See how Isaiah's words about idolatry can so easily be transposed to our way of life: 'He (man) plants a cedar, and the rain nourishes it. Then it becomes fuel for a man. He takes a part of it and warms himself, he kindles a fire and bakes bread; also he makes a god and worships it, he makes it a graven image and falls down before it. Half of it he burns in the fire; over the half he eats flesh, he roasts meat and is satisfied, also he warms himself and says, "Aha I am warm, I have seen the fire." And the rest of it he makes into a god, his idol; and falls down to it and worships it; he prays to it and says, "Deliver me for thou art my god." They know not, nor do they discern; for he has shut their eyes so that they cannot see, and their minds so that they cannot understand. No one considers, nor is there knowledge or discernment to say, 'Half of it I burned in the fire, I also baked bread on its coals, I roasted flesh and have eaten; and shall I make the residue of it for an abomination? Shall I fall down before a block of wood?" He feeds on ashes, a deluded mind has led him astray and he cannot deliver himself or say, "Is there not a lie in my right hand?"' (Is. 44:14–20).

Isaiah is stressing that though material possessions are important to man as a part of God's overall creation, they must not be asked to do something that they cannot do. They must not be given a value that they do not possess. They must not be worshipped as something that will give an answer to life, when such an answer is to be found only in God himself. Anyone who mistakenly makes possessions into idols must be laughed at with the derision he deserves. Just as in a primitive society one cannot expect wood for the fire to give peace of mind, neither can one expect unlimited wealth to do it in today's society. One of the main reasons why Jesus came to this earth was to proclaim that the time was at hand 'when the true worshippers will worship the Father in spirit and in truth' (John 4:23). When asked by the rich ruler (Luke 18:18–30) how to enter the Kingdom Jesus replied that he would have to give up his riches; Jesus wanted to show the man that to worship God truly it is necessary to place scant value on the material possessions that so often take God's place. To give away that wealth would then become a sign that the man was free from the control of the idol of materialism and the ties of the world and could worship the Father in spirit and in truth. Jesus knew that man cannot serve God and Mammon, and he knew that the only way to be sure of not serving Mammon is to give away things of Mammon. Such action would mean: a) that the person was not over-dependent on money or possessions for his satisfaction in life, and b) that the person was prepared to obey God regardless of the cost involved in human and practical terms.

Few rich people, even the righteous, are capable of such renunciation. 'How hard it is for those who have riches to enter the Kingdom of God. For it is easier for a camel to go through the eye of a needle than for a rich man to enter the Kingdom of God.' Nevertheless it was this kind of commitment that Jesus was looking for. He was uncompromising in his demands on anyone wishing to follow him. Not only did the person have to be prepared to forsake his family for his faith; and be prepared to carry his own cross and give up his life for his faith; but he also had to be prepared to let go of his personal possessions as well for the sake of Christ (cf. *Good News to the Poor*, pp. 27–8).

Not only does placing a particularly high value on material possessions cut man off from his creator, it also cuts him off from his fellow men by blinding him to someone else's poverty, and even becoming the cause of that poverty.

Jesus condemned also the holding of possessions if they were obtained through injustice. Zacchaeus had only to look into Jesus' eyes to know that it was not right for him to hold onto money that he had extorted from others unjustly. James states quite clearly the evil of such behaviour. 'Come on now you rich.... You have laid up treasure for the last days. Behold the wages of the labourers who mow your fields; which you kept back by fraud, cry out, and the cries of the harvesters have reached the ears of the Lord of hosts. You have lived on this earth in luxury and in pleasure, you have fattened your hearts in a day of slaughter; you have condemned, you have killed the rightous man; he does not resist you.' James 5:1–6. The accumulation and worship of material possessions can still be intricately related to the suffering of others even if the links in the chain are not always clearly visible in a complex society such as our own.

It was not because Jesus was against prosperity and wealth, that he spoke as he did about the rich. It is worth quoting the same principle in the present day from Archbishop Camara of Brazil. 'I used to think, when I was a cild, that Christ might have been exaggerating when he warned about the dangers of wealth. Today I know better. I know how very hard it is to be rich and still keep the milk of human kindness. Money is a dangerous way of putting scales on one's eyes, a dangerous way of freezing people's hands, eyes, lips, hearts.' (*Revolution through Peace*, pp. 142–3).

As has been pointed out earlier, E. F. Schumacher (*Small is Beautiful*, Chapter 3) has clearly described the way in which economic factors have become one of the most dominant influences in decision-making, how narrow we have become in our thinking. Other aspects that affect the quality of life such as beauty, health, cleanliness and peace are made subservient to economics, and are often respected only if they have an economic as well as an intrinsic value. In other words we have come to look at life through a very restricting pair of economic spectacles.

Jesus set us a clear example when personally confronted by a moral choice. At the start of his ministry, the devil tempted him to make stones into bread thereby satisfying the intense hunger that forty days of fasting had brought. But Jesus refused, answering: 'Man shall not live by bread alone but by every word that proceeds from the mouth of God' (Mt. 4:4). Jesus knew that neither he nor man could find fulfiment by the satisfaction of bodily needs alone; true satisfaction can come only from contemplating the whole nature of God, and trying to understand his revelation to us in creation, in the Bible, and in personal encounter. Only when we are thus satisfied will we be able to worship truly.

A Radical Christian Alternative

The church rests at ease in the world of the spirit because this world is so conveniently divorced from that of reality in which so many suffer poverty, hunger and injustice. But such a *spiritual* understanding of the nature of God separates the church from the practical outworking of Christian belief so that it never needs to face God's concern for justice for the poor, or how this should manifest itself in its own life and work. The church has ignored the stark incompatability between the message of the Bible, and the way it has chosen to interpret that message.

However, if we are serious about our faith this kind of dichotomy must be eradicated, starting with *criticism*, and following with *example*. The values of the new Kingdom must emerge for all to see, and the church must start to recognise itself as a body totally distinct from this present world order, with very different aims, objectives and methods; while still being intimately involved in this world just as Jesus was. So the first step the church must take is to divorce itself from society's basic principles and presuppositions.

The second step that the church must take to fulfil its role is to set an example. It must begin to live the Gospel that it proclaims, and its interior structure must reflect its message. It will be only when the Church practices the biblical principles that it preaches that it will be seen as taking seriously the new values of the new Kingdom, and it will then assume its true role of torchbearer.

Note

However an alternative thesis has been recently put forward by Conrad Boerma in his book *Rich Man, Poor Man and the Bible*. In it he traces the emergence and growth of poverty in the Bible and the various responses against it. He argues that poverty emerged in Israel's history with the change from communal or tribal ownership to private ownership, with the structures that developed around the monarchy, and with the growth of a class of wealthy landowners, business men and court officials. He sees communal ownership and stewardship under God, rather than private ownership under stewardship, to be the system true to the righteousness of the Covenant, and that which discourages poverty. He takes this on into the New Testament with the communal living of the New Testament church, and argues that herein lies the Christian norm.

CHAPTER SIX

Where do we go from here?

'The Christian will care less for the world, and at the same time more for the world, than the person who is not a Christian. He will not lose his heart to it – but he may lose his life for it' (*Epistle to Diognetus*).

Any consideration of revolution must include the whole programme of change from the unjust state of affairs, through the resultant unrest, upheaval and turmoil, on to the establishment of a new and better state, with its new values and aims. So far within this study we have recognised the persistence of inequality and injustice at local, national and international levels, and the church's connivance at that state of affairs. We have taken a fresh look at some central themes in the Bible, as they relate to both inequality and injustice. But to outline what is wrong, and why, is not enough. We must develop ideas about how change could be effected, and how Christian and biblical principles could be more effectively implemented.

In this chapter I hope to outline practical suggestions for a new approach within the church towards inequality and injustice. Applying new ideas will require breaking down old structures that serve no Christian purpose, searching for new attitudes towards ministry, mission, and service, and building new more flexible structures that will proclaim, in themselves, the message that Christians believe and follow. How much to break down and the cost involved, what to build in its place, the vision and faith required so that the church can live by biblical principles not compromise with those of secular society, so that the Kingdom of God can grow and develop despite the power of evil in the world – these are the points that need to be weighed up in relation to each practical suggestion. Yet our faith requires us to face this if we are to be at all true to the calling of Christ, his church, and his Word. We will look first at the two major areas of change; that of the church's own structure, and that of the church's relationship with society, and then go on to work out both of these in a new approach to ministry and mission in the church.

1. A New Example by the Church to Society

Let us begin our reconstruction by considering where changes ought to occur within the church's structure and attitudes. Any radical change must start in the heart if it is to have any real effect, and must develop into the will if it is going to avoid being superficial.

i) *Repentance*

If we accept the findings of earlier chapters, we must accept that the church has failed miserably in its primary task, of following in the steps of its master, because of its identification, not with the poor, as Jesus did, but with the powerful and wealthy. What steps are to be taken?

The first step must obviously involve *recognising* past failure and *admitting* it has started from the wrong side. It will not be enough to say sorry, and promise not to do it again, to make a big show of repentance and then go no further. It must analyse accurately the society of which it is a part, study its dynamics and morality as well as its own historical role within it. It will be only when the church faces this that it will ever understand the extent of its involvement, and the depth of its commitment to unbiblical and dehumanising ideas over a long period of time. And the more it analyses society and its involvement in it in the light of biblical attitudes towards the poor, needy and oppressed, the more it will come to recognise the depth of its own guilt.

It is possible to change sides before it is too late – but the size of the step and the implications involved, must not be underestimated. It can be taken, but it will involve a totally new, revolutionary stance. However, if we believe in the message of the Christian faith, then we will take this step; for we will know that the future of the faith and of mankind is at stake.

Of course, it will not be a purely intellectual, or theological step; that is what makes it so large. In order to change from adherence to an oppressive ideology to standing side by side in solidarity with those who have been exploited, we must recognise the reality of life that the oppressed have to live and must therefore not be satisfied until that reality is changed, and exploitation eradicated. That step, therefore, will demand a realignment of the whole church; all its people and all its assets. It will involve a reconsideration of the church's ideology and administration, its position within society and the renunciation of that position in its present form. The church has aligned itself with the rich, and those who oppress, instead of with the poor whom Jesus stood by, and so the change of attitude, approach and action required is equally comprehensive.

The next move will be to repent. We can go no further until we are deeply penitent and ask for forgiveness. It is essential that, as well as recognising the extent of our guilt, we should also repent fully of it. What does repentance involve? True repentance will always involve both words and action, both the admittance of failure, and the commitment to put things right. So repentance on this issue will demand a practical commitment to move from a position of wealth and power to a position of poverty, thus closing the gap between our theological belief and historical practice, between the lives lived by many church members and the life that the majority of mankind faces. It will involve relating our understanding of our faith to the humanisation of the world, and not just to the humanisation of the élite, and admitting that much of our wealth and power has been obtained by means unbecoming to the Christian faith, and then dispensing with such wealth. The challenge to the church will be the same as the challenge set to the rich young ruler by Jesus: 'Go, sell all your belongings and give them to the poor, and *then* come and follow me.'

It will mean a return to the message of Jesus as he described it at Nazareth, preaching the Good News to the poor, proclaiming the release of captives, liberty to the oppressed, sight to the blind, and the acceptable year of the Lord (i.e. the coming of the Kingdom of God). This will need to be worked out in a new appreciation of the meaning of the word 'love'. Love will no longer be the subject of 'idealistic subjectivistic and sentimental distortions' as Bonino puts it, but rather a commitment to work, with the help of God, towards the overthrow of the egotistical élitist dominance within mankind and the growth of human values.

God's word to Moses, to Joshua, David, Isaiah, Ezekiel, and Nehemiah showed a love for his people, that always involved action in history. God's word through his leaders was never simply theoretical: not only did he say to the Israelites after the Red Sea crossing that he had a future for them, he also led them to a new land. Our love today must always be rooted and grounded in reality, which may of course lead to conflict. Conflict is certainly not incompatible with love. Where love and justice are spoken of, conflict is bound to ensue. Love, as Jesus understood it, will involve us with injustice, judgement and conflict, if the world that we know today is as alien to the church now as it was to Jesus in his day.

ii) *A New Medium*

Not only will the church have to change the attitudes of its *heart* in repentance but it must also ensure that changes are made to its image. The church people see is speaking with two voices: the structure, the organisation, the image is saying one thing, while the message is claiming something quite different. Marshall McLuhan's famous phrase 'The medium is the message', sums up the dilemma facing the church. For, if the medium is the message, and if the medium is not a true reflection of the message, then the true message of the Christian Faith is not being communicated. Let us see what this means.

The message that must be communicated is the life, death and resurrection of Jesus Christ. Jesus was the servant of man in everything he did, from the stable where he was born, to the borrowed grave where he was buried. It follows then that the church as his body, his witness in today's world, should follow that pattern of witness.

Yet when we look at the medium, the structure of the church, we find that this structure just does not follow such an example. The church as an establishment is not radiating the message that Jesus both proclaimed and lived by. Of course it can be admitted that it is always the first to offer charity to those who are in need. It has always remembered and helped the poor, but from its own position of strength. It has not been in the position of the woman giving her last farthing; but rather in the position of the rich man giving part of his riches, paternalistically. Individual Christians down the ages have been like the widow. But the structure of the church itself, ever since its acceptance by the Roman State, has become identified with the élite in society, thus falling into a trap of its own making, that McLuhan's dictum helps us to understand.

The implications of such a contradiction are extremely important and must be borne in mind as possible changes are considered. As long as the structure of the church does not live out the message it proclaims, then the message it proclaims will not be truly understood, or believed, particularly by the poor and the deprived, for whom it was intended. This may well explain why the church in England has made so little ground amongst working people since the Industrial Revolution. Those who 'have not', have noticed the contradiction between the message and the structure, and have not been fooled by it. Consequently they have rejected its claim to be an 'answer to life', as being hypocritical. On the other hand many of the middle and upper classes have accepted the Christian faith but without really understanding the full significance of Christ's identification with those in need. So the dichotomy between the church's message and its structure has led one part of society to reject it completely, and another part to accept it in a perverted form.

Secondly, society will take notice of what the church says only when it can see a living example of the message. It will take notice only when it can see both the personal behaviour of the members, and the actual structure and outworking of the church, conforming to the message that it proclaims. When society sees that, then it will be far more likely to consider whether the message of Christ has any relevance to its own serious predicament.

Thirdly, as long as the Christian church seeks to spread its challenging and often unpopular message while itself remaining unreformed it is in danger of collapse and disintegration. Peter Berger (in *A Rumour of Angels*) talks about the church being a 'cognitive minority'; a small group of people who hold views that are very different from the majority in society. He goes on to say that for any cognitive minority to maintain its position, it has to be very clear about its basic principles. If there is any uncertainty or division within the minority, then the strength of the majority view will split it apart. Hence our fear that the church in its present form will not be able to survive, since it is neither certain of nor unanimous concerning its principles. The fact that many church members do not realise this makes matters worse as the pressure from society continues to mount, and forces the church into an increasingly compromised and isolated way of life.

Having noted both the contradiction that exists within the church, and some of the implications that follow from it, we now need to look at the internal structures and organisation to see where changes could and should be made. Repentance and response can then be demonstrated by changes which express the idea of repentance in practical ways. Such changes should lead also to a far deeper communication of the essence of the Gospel, and a more effective example of the Gospel being manifested to society at large.

a) Structures. As we look for new structures, we need to be aware of those failings in the present structures that have led to the medium not reflecting the message. As we have seen earlier, one of the major mistakes that the church made was to model its own organisation on a traditional social pattern (that of the Roman Empire around AD 300); rather than looking for a pattern that reflected its biblical message, it borrowed a structure from a totally secular source. So the Roman hierarchical or pyramidical structure has become accepted as the norm, and the church has been organised into areas or groups just as the Empire was divided into areas ruled by governors, etc. Such a decision at an early stage in the church's life, has had profound implications on the structure of our present church.

The church today has been overtaken and controlled by a kind of 'dynamic conservatism' (see *Beyond the Stable State*, Chapter 2 by Donald Schon, for a detailed analysis of this kind of position) being fully occupied in maintaining its structural status quo and seeing this as a perfectly valid and acceptable role. It has, as Schon would put it, 'a tendency to fight to remain the same'. It is saddled with buildings, organisations, commitments, and methods that were developed for a past age. This has led to the energies of the membership being increasingly taken up by the demands of an irrelevant superstructure with correspondingly less time being available for the more productive areas of church life. Responsibility for church fabric and finance can totally involve many of the key leaders of a church. Church life can so easily revolve round a dreary, cold, unwelcoming 600-seater Victorian structure used regularly by only thirty people, or around the upkeep of a historic monument which has to be kept going, not because it is a Christian place of worship, but purely because it is a good example of a certain school of architecture, or because it is 400 years old. Little wonder that congregations committed to such tasks often become totally alienated from the life that the rest of the population experience. This involvement leaves very little time for the basic task of the church – to pass on the Good News of Jesus Christ. It leads in the end to the death of many people's faith, for they see only a crumbling structure, and no encouragement for the future generations to grow in the faith. They think God is as dead as some of the buildings he is supposed to inhabit. Such church life leads to a ghetto mentality, and a retreat into the areas where church life is most easily continued – i.e. the middle-class suburbs and eclectic student churches. The church, because of its dynamic conservatism, has become satisfied with presiding over its own elaborate and time-consuming funeral service.

New structures should be more *biblically* based in that they should reflect the ideas about the Body of Christ which are found in the New Testament. The present hierarchical/pyramidical structures of Roman Catholicism and the Church of England in particular, have little to commend them. The early church appeared to favour the idea of a communion of brethren rather than a pyramid. Members within the communion had jobs that suited their gifts, but the different gifts were not ranked in specific order of importance. Christ was given the headship and all other members were seen as different parts of the body, all needed but none more needed than any other. True there were leaders; bishops and deacons, but leadership was seen only as one of the many gifts exercised by members of the body. Churches were often founded by travelling missionaries, but leadership was then quickly taken over by local people. Leaders appeared to arise from within the communion of believers rather than be imposed from without. There were, of course, guidelines as to the kind of person who ought to be encouraged into a position of leadership. The emphasis was on a man's spiritual maturity, rather than any academic background he might have. The original leaders, except Paul and Luke, certainly had no academic background. They would mainly have been called manual workers in today's terminology.

The early church seemed to grow like an amoeba with cells dividing, moving here and there, developing into new areas all the time. It was also very dependent on the leadership of the Spirit, and the advice and maturity of faith of the Apostles (advice still with us through the New Testament). It was fundamentally different from the bureaucratic organisation of church life today. The members, as well as the leaders, appear to have been far more aware of one another's needs, and so the life and growth of the organism reflected the local situation. If one member suffered, all suffered with him. If one member was elated, the rest rejoiced as well. The structure was not top heavy but reflected experience and maturity of faith at all levels. Authority certainly was a key word in the structure, but was based on the teaching of Ephesians 5: 24 – 'Be subject to one another out of reverence for Christ'.

Clearly the early church and our own highly complex administration are very different. It would not be right or possible suddenly to give up our bureaucracy for the New Testament church pattern overnight, for the two societies and their environment are very different. Yet there may well be some key principles to be found in the New Testament patterns that have long since been forgotten, that could be implemented in today's church with very positive results.

WHERE DO WE GO FROM HERE? 103

How? What Shape?

New structures should be geared to *cope with our fast changing society*. The Christian faith expresses a real paradox that must never be forgotten. On the one hand God in Christ is changeless, immortal, the one absolute being; yet on the other hand he is always changing, always different, like the many different facets of a diamond. He is the One True God, yet he speaks to different people, in different times, in different ways. As soon as God is seen to be a rigid person demanding static, pre-arranged responses, faith dies. For God offers one thing to one situation, and another to a different situation. The church therefore in its structure has to be able to express such flexibility. As the pace of change in society increases God needs to be seen as one who himself responds and who can help others to respond to those changes. The church's structures should reflect that same ability to adapt to the changes of environment and technology. It is not that Christians should conform to these changes but that they should express God's unchanging truth to a fast changing world in a way that can be understood by those who are mesmerised by such changes.

Clearly a pyramidical and bureaucratic structure is inadequate. Certainly the New Testament patterns which had to adapt to so many different cultures and environments during the first century (from corrupt Corinth to persecution-orientated Rome) and survived, would appear to be far more hopeful. Donald Schon has suggested other structures (cf. *Beyond the Stable State*) that are more suitable to learning and growth in times of rapid change, such as the youth movement styles of the sixties (where groups move and change shape like an amoeba according to needs or interest) or the idea of the 'constellation' (where there is one centre like the sun, and many satellite groups all circling round and being influenced by it). But we must beware of changing one structure that originated from a traditional social pattern for another that is recommended for situations of rapid social change. Even as we look for new structures, we must be sure that they reflect God's ability to speak afresh to a new or different environment, without betraying his eternal changeless character.

Grass roots approach

New structures should also be *strongest at the local level* rather than at the hierarchical and organisational level. As we have seen the biblical pattern certainly reflected this. Structures should reflect the people within a group rather than the other way round. At present a congregation, in its worship, in its administration, in its authority, reflects the model given to it by the past, rather than creating a model that derives from its own personal experience of Christ. The structure of a church should move from individual Christian experiences onwards, rather than downwards from an anachronistic pyramid of tradition. Such a movement would stimulate worship, leadership, teaching, and authority, to a far greater degree than is ever experienced today.

There could be helpful discussion on this point between the denominations. There is a great deal of difference in approach between the Established Church and the non-conformist churches, such as the Christian Brethren, the Pentecostal and the black churches. Although there are disadvantages in the more congregational approach, from among all the different approaches new patterns, new structures could emerge that would not sacrifice stability, maturity and spirituality and yet would reflect a far more spontaneous expression of Christian life that arose from the hearts of the members themselves.

Finally, new structures should *reflect the needs and the culture of the people* whom the church seeks to serve. Up till now it has maintained a culture of its own (basically middle class) that it imposes upon its adherents regardless of their culture or background. But God accepts people as they are, within their own culture. He does not expect people to change cultures when they become Christians, or break away from their upbringing because it does not coincide with the culture of the church. It should be possible to remain as faithful to a working-class background and be a Christian as it is to remain faithful to a middle-class background and be a Christian. New structures will need to make it far more possible for cultural differences to be maintained and encouraged rather than quietly discouraged. Structure will need, whilst encouraging unity, not to insist upon uniformity as well, as if they were one and the same thing. Far too often Christian structures have demanded uniformity of culture as an essential element in church life.

If a greater variety of culture, background, and environment is to be encouraged then it will have to be encouraged at the level of clergy training as well as at congregational level. No longer can the church afford to be dominated by middle-class intellectuals, where public school and university education is the rule rather than the exception. Emphasis must be put on encouraging local leadership into the full-time ministry regardless of social or academic background. Different methods of training must be developed to enable people from non-academic cultures to be welcomed into full-time leadership roles so that they can bring their experience of local cultures into the leadership and structures of the church.

There also needs to be a clearer distinction between Christian values and middle-class values. For many of our present church structures are influenced by values that are middle class and not necessarily Christian. Often middle-class values and Christian values have been thought to be synonymous, but they should not be. This too has had a detrimental effect on Christian structure and needs to be reconsidered in any radical re-appraisal.

b) Wealth. Down the centuries the church has accumulated a massive 'common fund'. By not redistributing it directly, it has used it to build up its own empire. Some of this empire is used for the benefit of other people (e.g. in education, social facilities, etc.) but the main part it uses for itself (e.g. churches, buildings, investments, etc.). So the Church of England and the Roman Catholic Church especially but also to a lesser degree the non-conformist churches have become involved in a very large business concern. The Church Commissioners alone own over £664 million in agricultural and commercial property holdings, and over £612 million in investments. Annual income from its investments now total over £56 million per year (cf. *Church Commissioners' Report* 1979). The church has become as big a business as many other large multinational industrial companies. Therefore the question must arise – did Jesus expect such a powerful business interest to grow out of his body and witness in the world? Surely not, for the image of Jesus and his life-style are intrinsically different from the image of the present day church and its accrued wealth. The church is not in existence to make money, yet it has invested its wealth in the capitalist system. This has meant accepting the system, regardless of whether it is good or bad by Christian standards, and having got involved in such an enterprise, it finds it extremely difficult to get out, because the monies given by people in the past for Christian purposes, rather than going to people in need, are actually used for the upkeep of the internal structures of the church, and the payment of the clergy. Individual churches are using money originally donated for charitable purposes for the upkeep of their structure instead of using it to serve other people. In the New Testament, however, each church was normally self-sufficient in caring for buildings used and paying its full-time leaders.

The balance of individual wealth within the membership of the Body of Christ must also be considerable. Evidence can be drawn from the New Testament to show that present Christian attitudes towards our personal wealth and how we use it run contrary to principles developed by the early church. This has been discussed in detail by R. Sider (*Rich Christians in an Age of Hunger*, Chapter 4), but some simple examples give a clear indication of present deviations from the New Testament patterns. It seems that there was then a very real concern for the wholeness of the Body of Christ, that we have since lost, and fellowship certainly included economic sharing. The principles behind their economic attitudes sprang from the teachings of Jesus: 'Seek first his kingdom and his righteousness, and all these things shall be yours as well' (Mt. 6: 33). The church today does not have the same detachment from material possessions, and neither are individual members generally prepared to share their surplus with those members of the body who are in need. Compare for instance the wealth of Christians in the West with their counterparts in the Third World; or the life-style of Christians in the English city commuter belts with Christians living in the inner city. If the church wishes to set a real example to society it will need not only to redistribute its institutional wealth but there will also need to be real sharing and redistribution between individual members and individual churches within the Body of Christ. Only by the example of such sharing will the real message of love and brotherhood be expressed.

c) Buildings. The church is extremely well endowed with property of all types, in nearly every part of the country: itself owning churches, schools and colleges, youth clubs, community centres, old people's homes, clergy houses, and owning other types of property and land that are rented out.

There are places where the church building admirably suits the needs of its own particular area. Usually, however, the buildings no longer meet the needs of those who use them. The reasons for this vary but often a church is far too big, dark, dreary and impossible to heat economically, and by its aspect and size does not encourage genuine Christian worship and fellowship. Often the cost of the upkeep of the building is crippling, or even impossible for the congregation to pay. There may be far too many churches serving one area. These conditions have existed for a very long time, and yet the church, both at the local and national level, has soldiered on and changes have been made only in a few individual cases. Surely the time has come for it to cut its losses, and reduce its buildings to a more manageable size. Church life must determine buildings, rather than let itself be dominated by them.

Surely the essence of the Christian faith is that people matter more than anything else and certainly more than buildings. And the church is not, as is so often assumed, a building, or even a group of people meeting in a building: it is a group of people. When the place of meeting becomes too important to that group, then its faith begins to suffer. It may well be worth noting the fact that, in the days before the church had its own particular buildings (i.e. the first 300 years after Christ) it grew faster than at any other time in its history. The time has come to re-structure the church ruthlessly according to the needs and expectations of the present, to sell off what is not needed, and to become far more flexible in what is needed. The church must use multi-purpose buildings that attract rather than those that discourage the fellowship it is proclaiming. A building that *is* in keeping with the theme of the Gospel, is the home. Far greater use could be made of the idea of house churches, which were used in New Testament times, thus drastically cutting the effort, and cost, of church upkeep and leaving congregations free to witness through their preaching of the Word and their service to others. For larger church meetings, halls could be hired when needed, or when a number of house churches wanted to meet together. There is no real need for the church to own the buildings it uses; without them many would be freed for other kinds of service. Is the church's unwillingness to dis-encumber itself a sign that it is afraid of New Testament Christianity?

The inner city areas are probably the most deprived areas in the country, but it is just here that there is often a considerable amount of church plant, much of which is incredibly under-used. The population density in these areas is often extremely high and land is at such a premium that there are very few community facilities available in spite of the great number of people; the church owns property which is hardly used and there is a community of people in desperate need who are not able to use the potential facilities in the area, because the church won't let them. What hypocrisy! No wonder no one in such an area thinks twice about Christianity; the church says, 'Jesus loves you', but at the same time, 'I won't give you what I know you desperately need'. It must be prepared either to sell/give such property to the community/council, or at least make it as fully available as possible. Then the buildings will be seen to reflect a little of Jesus' concern for those in need.

Having admitted and repented of the mistakes of the past, the church must respond by changing radically. She need never be frightened by the size and immensity of the task, for she knows that her message is one that can work miracles – even on structures and bureaucracies.

2. Change in the Church's Relationship to Society

i) *Blanket Support of Society*

We need to demand a change in the church's overall attitude to society, its social structure and the power structures. There is now, and in the past there has been, general agreement that secular society is fundamentally reasonable, so no real Christian critique of it has emerged. There has been a kind of 'blanket acceptance'. When there has been disagreement it has always been within the framework of this overall acceptance. The church has in a sense dealt only with the weaknesses of a sub-Christian society, rather than the root cause of those weaknesses. Christians can no longer be content with working out a personal expression of their faith, in terms only of their own daily experiences. They need to realise that God's Kingdom can be encouraged and extended, not only by personal witness, but also by changing the structures in society that offend, and run contrary to, the values of the Kingdom.

Dis-establishment for the Church of England would be essential for any radical re-appraisal to be carried out; it would need to be done at every level, from personal and local, to national and global, from values, presuppositions, aims and expectations to the out-workings in practical terms, from the past historical context to the possible choices for the future. It would mean that, rather than looking to our traditional social structure for a pattern upon which to build our interpretation of Christian values, we would compare basic human experience with the biblical attitudes to the same issues, to find a more adequate and flexible basis on which to build a society worthy of the Kingdom of God.

The church must speak clearly and decisively on such issues *now*, otherwise it will lose even more of the confidence of humanity as a whole. As President Nyerere of Tanzania has put it 'Unless the Church ... expresses God's love for man by involvement and leadership in constructive protest against the present conditions of man, then it will become identified with injustice and persecution. If this happens, it will die ... because it will then serve no purpose comprehensible to modern man' (*Freedom and Development*, p. 216, Speech on 'The Church and Society').

As Brian Wren says in *Education for Justice* (p. 64) people who are in a position of privilege find it hard to realise that their 'privilege might be held at the cost of other people's suffering'. He goes on to use an example from a news magazine printed during the Vietnam war where a cartoon strip carried the following captions. 'I only work on the assembly line – I only drive a delivery truck –

I only take delivery of the goods – I only help to load the plane – I only give clearance for take-off – I only pilot an aircraft – I only press a button.' The last picture showed Vietnamese villagers saying 'And we get killed by the bomb'. If we are part of a society that deprives many of their full share of human potential and human resources; and if we belong to that part of society that receives more than an equal share of what is available; then by remaining silent about the system that allows such a state of affairs, and even enforces its continuance, we are party to injustice, as clearly as if we mugged an old lady in the street. Structures can very easily hide the source of injustice but if we are to be as committed to eradicating injustice as God calls us to be then we will need to unravel the thread that runs through the structure of the system, find where the responsibility lies, and eliminate the evil.

Christians have often been unaware of injustice within society because they have lived segregated lives, just as surely as black and white live apart in South Africa. People who live in an exclusive suburb just cannot comprehend what it is like to be an unmarried mother on the twenty-third floor of a tower block in inner London, or to have the next flat's lavatory noises waking you up in the morning, or to have cockroaches in the cavity of the walls of your flat for four years with the landlord doing nothing about it. They do not know what it is like to be unemployed or to be living on the edge of the poverty line. Christians are frequently unaware of the way in which the structures from which they benefit cause others considerable hardship. But there is also a sense in which ignorance is deliberate or perhaps someone who is very well off is fully aware of the injustice of a particular situation. That knowledge may make him feel guilty. He may try to forget or avoid it, or he may just say that it is part of the system and that you cannot change the system. Or he may say – 'Well if that person used his initiative he could get out of trouble just like me.' Deep down, however, he probably knows that in one way or another he is partly responsible – but that to change the injustice will mean to change the system, and to change the system may mean that he will lose out, so that the sufferer can be relieved – and that is what he does not want to do. He, of all people, knows the truth of Dr. Charles Birch's statement 'The rich must live more simply that the poor may simply live'. Facing injustice is a costly business for those who are receiving more than their fair share. That is why those who control our society, and benefit from it, oppose change. But there is no reason why the Christian church should continue to conform to, and even condone, such behaviour.

Both economically and socially the church receives benefits from its close integration with the state, benefits which would cease with dis-establishment. These beneficial arrangements are of various kinds. Many people – including many members of the church – are not even aware of their existence. But they are none the less real for that. And they would be at risk if the relationship between church and state were to be modified. There are also social benefits to be enjoyed; certain Bishops automatically have a seat in the House of Lords, and the clergy are still given status, and often positions of authority in society, by virtue of their position in the church. In the field of education, although the church runs its own schools, the state pays for their administration, leaving the church free to exert considerable power which it would not automatically have in a state system. Without state support, however, it would be unlikely that the church could afford to run these schools.

There are also issues between church and state over the considerable plant that the church owns. When, recently, Parliament considered taxing all buildings and land sold in an attempt to share more equally the value of land and property, the church was the first to complain, as it stood to lose so much, and the delay in the implementation of that Bill could well be attributed, in part, to pressure by the church. There is also the question of the church's status as a 'charity' – if it were to lose this status, it is unlikely it would be able to continue with many of its commitments. Let us not forget that when the church did speak clearly to the state by its witness, in its early days, it was not rewarded by being called a charity, but was persecuted continuously. There are of course many other examples of this unseen support of the church by the state, but let these serve.

The established church is also linked legally with the state – sometimes not to its own advantage. The state still has the power to appoint bishops and has to ratify in Parliament any changes in the established church's internal structures. How different from the New Testament church which was locally autonomous. If the church is to be free to analyse and criticise what is wrong in society it must become disentangled from the state, for if it begins to criticise the state more forcefully, the state might react by not appointing leading critics to positions of responsibility where they could have even more effect. The church will have to be prepared to break such links, however much it loses out in certain respects, so that it can be a free body; free to preach and follow the commands of Christ and to proclaim them clearly to an unbelieving society.

This collusion between the élite, the powerful and the church is also present in individual Christians who have vested interests in the status quo just as much as the church as an institution. In general a very high proportion of church membership comes from the middle and upper classes whose earnings and inherited wealth are both well above the national average. Their educational opportunities and living conditions are far better than the majority of the population, and they have far more influence on the various aspects of society than the average man in Britain. Often they are leaders in government, in law, in education, in business, in land, in capital assets, in spending power. The majority of the church members belong to that group of people who govern rather than being governed. Questioning the rules could lead to unpopularity, ostracism or worse. Take an example from the business sector. If a Christian manager or director feels that the profits of an enterprise are not shared fairly between those who have invested their capital, those who work at a decision-making level, and those who work manually to produce the commodity, and that there is a need to redistribute the profits in the light of what he believes to be biblically just, what does he do? Often the Christian will compromise his principles and accept the power of the existing system. But that is flying in the face of biblical values. He ought to work for a fairer redistribution regardless of what his associates might say. The cost involved is enormous at a personal, let alone a structural, level.

ii) *Methods of changing society*

How do we inaugurate the changes which we feel are needed? In the past, the church has usually approached the subject of making changes in a rational, peaceful and conciliatory way. It has 'appealed' to the particular body, in a 'gentlemanly manner', to 'reconsider' its position in an 'enlightened and charitable' way. In terms of methods, the church has seen peace, conciliation, passivity, neutrality and objectivity as characterising a Christian approach; whereas it sees conflict, demand, violence, aggression, taking sides and withdrawal of support as being contrary to Christian values. However, our re-assessment of biblical values should make us question this judgement. For it can be argued that the former methods do not take injustice, deprivation, greed, and hate seriously enough. There are many instances in the Bible which show that when a conciliatory attempt to remove injustice fails, then confrontation becomes necessary. Certainly the ministry of the eighth-century prophets, of Moses with Pharaoh, and of Jesus himself, involved confrontation and actual aggression in the face of injustice. (Jesus overthrowing the money changers in the temple is the supreme example.) To take Jesus' message seriously, we must fight injustice and self-seeking to the end, until it is overthrown. There can be no room for conciliation and compromise, and the Kingdom of God cannot be built upon it. The Kingdom will be built on reconciliation, which means exchanging the new for the old and this may involve decisive confrontation, and conflict, which the church should not be afraid of, or attempt to avoid. This readiness to risk conflict in order to achieve God's justice will lead the church into a far more direct role in fighting injustice within society. It will mean taking sides when, so often, previously it has remained neutral. It will mean withdrawing support and labour instead of meekly 'appealing'. It will mean a commitment to fight on against injustice instead of giving in to the over-riding power of the élite that has so often quashed the church's resistance in the past.

The need for this more active and determined approach against oppression and injustice is shown to be absolutely necessary by Brian Wren (*op. cit.* pp. 60 ff). He quotes black American Frederick Douglass in his West Indian Emancipation Speech in 1857 saying 'Power concedes nothing without demand'. He goes on to argue that, in practice, no one in a position of power, wealth or property ever gives in, and shares out that power in a more equal fashion. No one gives up voluntarily what he has, even if it would mean greater equality, and a greater sense of justice, as the situation in Southern Africa demonstrates. Therefore, if anyone is concerned to bring about a state of greater justice he cannot expect the oppressor to give in freely: rather he must expect to enter into conflict until that state is achieved. If the church is truly against injustice it will be led into conflict; for ultimately there is no other way for justice to be achieved. If love is anything at all, it is a commitment to serve a person to the end, so love for deprived humanity will mean confrontation to the end. Jesus' ministry was a classic example of confrontation, with an overpowering structure. There was no sense of neutrality, or compromise, so ultimately he went to the cross. At present the church is nowhere near going to any cross, for it has not been prepared to enter into conflict with evil injustice and oppression, particularly those of state or institution. Christians who have been deported, or imprisoned in Southern Africa, and men like Martin Luther King, are exceptions, and the real example to follow. Their determination to confront evil shows that the Christian faith could oppose structural evil today, if only it recognised how central the issue is to the building up of the Kingdom of God.

However, it must not be forgotten that as well as fighting injustice the Christian is trying to hasten the Kingdom of God. Conflict for the Christian does not mean simply the overthrow of the oppressor. The Kingdom must come from a mutual desire to make the Biblical values a reality. This will mean that conflict and violence will need to be used very carefully, so that afterwards neither side will be blinded by fear and hate but each will realise the essential need for God's ideals of justice when working for true humanity, and for the Kingdom of God. This qualification does not weaken the importance of conflict as a tool for the Kingdom, it only shows how it must be viewed, in the light of Christ's attitude of acceptance of everyone who 'truly repents'. Conflict is to be used to draw people to repentance and not to chase them away from it.

iii) *Redistribution of Wealth in Society*

At present the structure of society ensures that the ratio between the richest 20% and the poorest 80% of the population remains stable. The same is true of Western Capitalist countries in relation to the poorer Third World countries, and will continue unless the church takes radical action.

This is an immense task. There have been political parties who have wanted to achieve such aims and who have failed, and there have been many who have wanted radical changes and who have ended up just 'tinkering' with the system. Change must occur at the right level for it is no use working for changes at lower levels when decision makers at higher levels can nullify those efforts at the stroke of a pen. Both the organised churches and individual Christians in positions of power and influence will have to work without thought for themselves so that wealth and economic power can be more fairly distributed. Christians have to become involved with other political groups working for the same ends. Such a liaison will need to be carefully thought out, but a combined effort on such an issue might well prove to be beneficial rather than detrimental. It is probable that the economic extremes of our society are far more deepseated than they were in Israel's society when plans for the Jubilee and Restoration were first mentioned, so there should be a great urgency about Christian action.

3. New Patterns of Ministry

i) *Identification with the Needy*

Many Church members have little experience of real deprivation, so a first condition of any new life-style will be that Christians must experience deprivation, suffering and injustice at first hand. For example, it might mean living in a deprived housing area, teaching in a local school, helping with legal aid, assisting in young offenders' after-care groups, helping in an inner city open youth club, or visiting geriatric wards. This would provide a measure of identification, and understanding, even though, to walk into an area of need, knowing that one can easily walk out and return to relative comfort if things become too difficult (the position of most clergy even in such areas) means that it would still be difficult to appreciate the intensity of deprivation experienced by someone who has no such means of escape.

The embarrassing fact for most Christians is that the example Jesus has set us does not let us rest with just going and experiencing deprivation for a short time to know what it is like. Jesus actually calls us to move towards a life of permanent identification with those in need.* The Christian faith does not challenge just clergy and a few social workers to go and live and work in areas of deprivation; it calls every member of its body to do so. This is where the real challenge of Christianity becomes personal. The practical logistics of such moves, of course, provide plenty of excuses (such as the shortage of houses in inner city areas, or – 'Should one inflict such pressures on one's family?') but they do not affect the principle, which has so far not been considered by the church as a whole; far less implemented. But we cannot escape Jesus' identification with those who were deprived, even to being crucified 'outside the city wall' with the outcasts. Somehow, a new structure for the church and a new life for Christians should lead to real identification with the needy. It may involve Christians giving up their position in society, their pleasant house and garden in the suburbs, their private schooling for the family, their accrued wealth, their dependence on finance as a way out of hardship, their lifelong friends, so that they can follow Jesus in practice and commit themselves to serving, and standing beside, those who are deprived of their basic human inheritance. There have been a number of examples of such commitment within church history, and they have had a profound effect. The time has come for these examples to cease to be the exception, and begin to be the rule. Mother Theresa should no longer remain an example at a distance, but an example of what each member of the church could do. The Salvation Army in its early days showed how a whole body of Christians could totally identify themselves with those in need. Their complete identification and witness in India, at that time, shows what can be done when

* See note on p. 125

Christians respond to Jesus' example to go out and serve the poor. No longer can the church be content with only a few of its members identifying with those in need, it must move as a body towards complete identification. Only through such costly sharing will the oppressive system ultimately be defeated.

ii) *Erosion of False Values*

If an increasing number of Christians begin to search and study God's words concerning the poor and deprived, then apply those principles to the present situation, and implement them within the life of the church and society, then values that are incompatible with the values of the Kingdom of God could be gradually eroded. This would entail being very clear about principles, accepting no compromise and being dissatisfied until practical changes had come about.

Those who gained this fresh understanding of Jesus' priority commitment to the poor and underprivileged would need to spend time sharing it with others and supporting one another so that the enthusiasm to implement such principles did not wane.

Donald Schon describes how 'erosion' can enable change to take place. A massive organisation such as the church is often controlled by a kind of 'dynamic conservatism' that stops any real or far-reaching changes from taking place, so that it is necessary gradually to build up the 'threshold for change', an ever increasing dissatisfaction with the present situation. Only then will there be sufficient power for radical changes to be made.

Such erosion of the old patterns will be needed at every level. Both the church as an institution and individual Christians within it will need to work for the introduction of such Kingdom values as justice, equality and prosperity. It will need to criticise the Government, and individual Christians in positions of influence will need to exert pressure in their respective fields. Christians involved in business, management, civil services, industrial relations, government programmes, social benefit programmes, and many other fields will need to speak clearly of what they believe. Individual Christians will need also to deepen their commitment to the deprived and strengthen their opposition to injustice. Christians should keep only what is basic to life, and give away their surplus to someone in greater need. For example when Wesley started his ministry, he found that £30 per year would cover his needs, so he gave away the surplus which was only a few pounds. Later, the sale of his books made him a rich man but he still lived on the £30 and gave all the rest away. Obviously, inflation and the needs of a family and household have to be taken into account, but even so, the principle behind the simpler life-style still holds firm for a Christian. If it is possible for many families today to live on a wage that is so low that they pay no income tax, then that is a challenge for all Christians to consider.

We must commit ourselves to simplicity, and witness that the luxuries of life are not as important as the Kingdom of God. It must be seen that Christians can give these up in order to alleviate someone else's distress. Such simplicity of living would have two direct effects: Christians would no longer be identified with the wealthy in society; and wealth would be available for those deprived of basic human necessities. It would set the example for a practical redistribution of wealth.

Such changes in life-style need not be limited to finance. The New Testament lays great emphasis on every member using his gifts for the benefit of the church and of people in need around. Therefore, not only should an individual's surplus wealth be available, but his gifts, however varied, should also be available for the service of the deprived. Whatever gifts a person has, there will always be someone who would be glad to receive the benefits of them and both the obvious and less obvious skills, present in most churches, could be shared out. Those involved in law could make their legal services available to those unfairly treated. Those in education could help in encouraging those in educational priority areas, particularly in helping them to become more aware of themselves. Those in health and welfare services could work in the more needy areas instead of seeking promotion, or the more remunerative side of the profession. Those who are eloquent (and any family argument will show up that skill) should find ways of speaking out for justice on particular human needs within the community. There will be a real need for Christians at every level of politics, from community action groups, tenants' associations, local councils, to national and parliamentary positions. Those who have experience of multi-cultural societies could commit themselves to fight racial discrimination which is becoming a major issue in certain areas of our cities. Those who relate well to teenagers, have plenty of scope to serve the needs of the many youngsters who are thrown into adult life full of feelings of inadequacy and uncertainty. When so much is said about teenage vandalism and soccer hooliganism, so much could also be done, simply by caring adults who make themselves available. It is not only professional people who have skills needed by society, as is so often thought. Everyone has a skill or a gift he can share. A helper for 'meals on wheels' can serve as well as the lawyer, doctor, or

Member of Parliament. It is not the type of gift that matters, it is whether it is applied to the situations of deepest need, injustice, and oppression. If every Christian gave priority to this kind of service when considering what to do with his job or career, his spare time, wealth and expertise, then both the structural and practical injustices within our society would be truly threatened. The erosion of the evils in our society by the members of the Kingdom of God is no easy task.

iii) *Setting the Agenda*

Christians seeking such a new way of life could so easily fall back into a pattern of 'do goodism', or 'paternalism', and do their 'own thing' without listening to those who are deprived, and without allowing them to set the agenda themselves as to what should be done – Christians will need to remember that for a long time they have been the ones to command, now they must stand back.

As Paulo Freire has pointed out (*Pedagogy of the Oppressed*), if there is to be any real change in a society where the balance of power and wealth gives rise to extreme poverty and injustice, then it must be initiated by *those who have been oppressed* rather than by those who have done the exploiting. If those who have been the oppressors initiate change, or set the agenda, then any changes suggested will be influenced by their previous ideological position, training, and circumstances. Such changes will always, consciously or subconsciously, reflect the background of those who have dominated and exploited rather than that of those who have been oppressed. And as any change that is worth the name must start where the exploited and 'used' man stands, it is only the exploited man who can initiate it, for only he truly knows what it is like to be there. It would be invalid for the church to repent, and then go about its own way of making amends. It would only, because of its own entrenched position, become guilty of some other form of oppression if it did not, first, go to those who are deprived, and ask them what ought to be done to enable a more fully human life to develop, one that is shared equally by all mankind.

It is important that Christians do not make the mistakes made in so many revolutions before. It is not the aim to change one form of oppression for another, with the new leaders becoming as oppressive as the old ones, though in different ways. This happens as soon as the new leaders lose touch with the needs which initiated the revolution in the first place. It is important for the church to see that in its repentance and action, it is not seeking a new answer within the oppressed/oppressor dynamic, but completely *outside* that dynamic, based on a concern for the full and equal humanisation of everyone. Surely this is God's plan for his creation, the purpose of Jesus' coming, and the task of the church today.

Let us look at the writings of Che Guevara. He, as a revolutionary leader (and doctor), lived through the Cuban revolution, which he describes in *Episodes of the Revolutionary War*. 'As a result of daily contact with these people (the local peasant farmers in Cuba) and their problems, we became firmly convinced of the need for a complete change in the life of our people (the guerillas). The idea of agrarian reform became crystal clear. *Communion with the people*, ceasing to be a mere theory, became an integral part of ourselves. Guerillas and peasants began to *merge into a solid mass*. No one can exactly say when, in this long process, the ideas became reality, and we *became part of* the peasantry. As far as I am concerned, the contact with my patients in the Sierra turned *a spontaneous and somewhat lyrical* decision into a *more serene force, one of an entirely different value*. Those poor, suffering loyal inhabitants of the Sierra cannot even imagine what a *great contribution they made to the forging of our revolutionary ideology*.' The church, in the same way, needs to take the message of Jesus, and standing side by side with people as Guevara did, allow that Good News to work its own miracle and transform both the church and the people into a completely new experience of Christian reality.

Freire, using Guevara as an example, comments (*op. cit.* p. 148): 'Instead of following predetermined plans, leaders and people, mutually identified, together create the guidelines of their action. In this synthesis, leaders and people are somehow reborn in a new knowledge, and new action.... The more sophisticated knowledge of the leaders is remade in the empirical knowledge of the people, while the latter is refined by the former. In cultural synthesis – and only in cultural synthesis – it is possible to resolve the contradiction between the world view of the leaders and that of the people, *to the enrichment of both*.'

Both the church then, and individual Christians, being leaders in the sense that they bear the Good News of Jesus Christ, will do full justice to the Good News only when they place it side by side with the experience of people who have been deprived, and allow the synthesis of the two to create an entirely new Christian response, nurtured in reflection, and growing into action.

iv) *Emancipation of the Oppressed*

The first step in the emancipation of an oppressed person is for him to appreciate what he could be. It will gradually dawn on him that he is deprived of life, not because he is inadequate, but because he is being unjustly treated. He will gradually begin to respond to his situation by saying, 'I am oppressed, I am unjustly treated, I am deprived of my humanity', rather than passively accepting his situation with the silent thought, 'I am inadequate' (cf. Brian Wren – *Education for Justice*, p. 81). When this realisation dawns, then the whole perspective changes. For then he realises that it is not all his fault that he is suffering in the way that he is, but that it is the fault of others, and of society; and that it is possible to put the fault right. The sufferer realises that he has been cheated of his birthright, and that it is up to him and his fellows to work to regain that birthright. This will lead on to a gradual change in attitude towards his environment. If he is encouraged, supported, and united with others who begin to realise the same facts, he will begin to fight those who are taking away his basic human rights. He will begin to oppose the structures that are causing the economic, psychological, and emotional oppression.

This appreciation, that it is not the personal inadequacies of people in areas of deprivation that has kept them in this condition but rather the distinct policies maintained by the structure of our society, has emerged from the work of the Home Office Community Development Project in their Interim and Final Reports. As one of the Coventry C.D.P. team suggests 'The problems of disadvantage, at the grass roots seem to have less to do with the internal pathology of particular families, or with lack of co-ordination in planning and implementation, than with basic inequalities in the distribution of incomes, jobs, housing and public goods and services'. (John Bennington – 'Are these the roots of social distress?' *Coventry Municipal Review*, July 1973). He argues from C.D.P. findings, that it is these inequalities, upheld by local and central government, that are maintaining families in an area such as Hillfields in the deprivation that enmeshes them. The Report even goes so far as to suggest that 'the growth and prosperity of other sectors of Coventry's life have depended on the maintenance of Hillfields as a run down area'. So, in the overall plan, the deprivation of some families has been seen as an acceptable cost involved in providing increased prosperity for others. They support this suggestion by detailing the way in which the area has been used for many years as a 'buffer against market uncertainties, by being a reservoir of labour for industry, a safety valve responding to fluctuations in public investment, and a fluid pool of land, with potential changes in use'.

If the above is a true example of the pressures exerted upon people living in deprived areas, and if it can be accepted that this example is typical of the experience of many of the deprived, then the emancipation of such oppressed people becomes paramount, not only for the sake of the people deprived themselves but also for the good of society as a whole. It can also be seen that any such emancipation will suceed only when it is based on those who are deprived recognising their situation, and joining together to demand the end of their oppression.

It is within the framework of such emancipation that the local church could have a decisive role, because of its underlying understanding of every person's God-given human rights of equality of opportunity. It could become a very real and positive catalyst to the situation by identifying with those in deprived circumstances and it could become available as an encourager and enabler to those seeking emancipation from such inequality. The church would have to recognise that kindness and 'ambulance-style' social work are not enough and that what is required is total emancipation. It would mean endorsing President Nyerere's view of the church's position. 'Kindness is not enough, piety is not enough, charity is not enough. The men who are now suffering from poverty ... need to be helped to stretch themselves; they need to be given confidence in their own ability to take control of their own lives' (*Freedom and Development*, p. 220).

Let us take one or two examples which illustrate the starting point from which such involvement and commitment could evolve. The Newham Community Renewal Programme has been working in the East End of London since 1970. Based on a Christian presence within the area, it has committed itself to serving the needs of the community. Its spheres of activity include the usual children's, youth, adult and old people's work, as well as the more specialist needs, such as Asian and West Indian work, and involvement based on a number of Community Centres. It seeks to balance its evangelistic concern with a deep social involvement in relevant issues. It is deeply committed to the needs of the powerless, and their dependence on the powerful. And in all its work it seeks to start where people are, using self-help and local leadership wherever possible, and encouraging the belief of individuals in their ability and power to affect and change their own physical and social environment. The result has been that ever since 1970 the Programme has grown into an ever widening sphere of influence within Newham, enabling and fostering small groups, concerned with various forms of social action, as the needs become evident.

It has sought to be of assistance particularly to minority groups within the Borough, enabling language and community groupings to develop among Asians, and looking into the reasons behind the considerable family breakdown, particularly between young people and their parents, amongst the West Indians. In all of this work the involvement has been at ground level, allowing the needs of the people to dictate the direction of the involvement. The chief concern has not been to question the social structure which is causing such hardship in the East End, but rather to show care and concern towards those affected. Yet there is also a growing awareness of the need for such action, with certain church leaders becoming involved in politics and speaking out clearly against the system.

Another example of grass roots involvement is the development and support of a local community newspaper in Camberwell called *Compass* (cf. *Urban Ghetto*, p. 71, D. Bartles-Smith and D. Gerrard). Started by a group of local clergy, but developed in close liaison with tenants' associations and leaders in the community, the paper has served a very real need in the area. It has a circulation of nearly one in three houses in the area, and has been used as a platform for bringing a number of local issues into the open. It has given people a deeper appreciation of the community to which they belong, and has encouraged the local residents to get together to get things done. It has published stories that bring to light the needs of elderly people; facts that show the inadequacy of the local political parties when it comes to getting things done; and a campaign aimed at reducing racial tension during a South African cricket tour. It has proved itself, in many instances, to be a very strong instrument, which can encourage and bring about changes needed in the local community. It is an example of the fact that, when people get together to fight injustice, then changes can take place. And it is a good example of the way in which church members can make themselves available to the needs of their community, and in so doing, help to bring about change that is necessary for the benefit of all.

A further example of the church's involvement in a particular aspect of local community life is the Deptford Festival. This Festival, run in Deptford for many years, is aimed at drawing members of the community together to enjoy themselves, over a two-week period in June each year. To begin with the clergy had a strong influence in the leadership, but now this is far more widely based in the community. Once again it has been a medium for encouraging local tenants' associations to do things for themselves. Activities, ideas and attempts to meet needs surfacing at the time of the Festival, often continue to operate in a modified manner through the year. The Festival, of course, does not function as an agent of direct political or social change in the way we have been considering earlier. Yet it does have a considerable influence on people's social lives, and encourages zestful enjoyment, something which should be an integral part of real living. Such local involvement could never be seen as the whole picture, but it is certainly one of the pieces of the jigsaw, and a piece that the church has so often mislaid.

Many have argued that it is at the point where the two sectors of production converge that inequality and injustice begin. If Christians wish to fight inequality at its roots they *must* become involved at this level. They must support those who seek a fair contract between investors of capital and their managers on the one hand, and those who provide labour on the other. They must strive for a fair distribution of the profits made by such an enterprise and for greater involvement in decision making by those who contribute their labour, to whom similar rights and privileges should be granted as to investment or management experts. If Christians do believe that all men should be allowed an equal chance to fulfil their God-given humanity, then they must work for such a fulfilment at the point where men come together to use their differing God-given talents to produce something.

A very good example of what can emerge from a labour force's interest and concern for the life of its company is the Alternative Corporate Plan put forward by the Lucas Aerospace Combine Shop Stewards' Committee (cf. *The Right to Useful Work* – Mike Cooley, 1978). This particular scheme was set up as a constructive alternative to redundancy. It suggests 150 or more new products that could be made by Lucas Aerospace in the existing plants, so reducing redundancy. All the ideas come from the existing work force. Some of them are products that would have a positive benefit to society, e.g. kidney machines, universal power packs for simple life-support systems, etc. Here then is a situation where members of a work force have got together positively and creatively to think and make suggestions. They have a concern to keep skilled men in employment, and that their company should produce useful products for the community.

Christians in these situations may find themselves working with others from very different ideological backgrounds, perhaps Marxists and atheists. Such united work could have many benefits and should not be seen as compromising. It is perfectly possible to share a common aim with another ideology without being absorbed or taken over by it. Indeed Christians need to be encouraged when certain values of God's Kingdom are shared by another ideology. It could even become common ground where others might come to see the Christian faith in a fresh light.

v) *Personal or Corporate Changes*
Should the changes we have discussed be encouraged within the corporate structure of the church, or should they be encouraged to develop within the life of the individual believer? Obviously there are some ideas that can be practised only by the corporate church, and some that can be done only by the individual. But there are considerable areas of ministry that can be done at either level.

In the past, the church has tended to set up the structure for such services and then asked its members to run them: education, family welfare, youth clubs, play schemes, old people's clubs, community centres, etc. The result has been that church life has been dominated by the support required for such social provision, often at the expense of the life and growth of the Christian Family. For although the two are not mutually exclusive the former can easily submerge the latter, because often the administration of such structured social provision makes demands on a church that the individual members find hard to meet. The result can be the subordination of the basic content of church life to the work of social provision; such basic aspects as the pastoral needs of the individual church members, the concern to pass on the Christian faith directly to other people, or the development of the worship life of the church, all suffer as they are subordinated to a structure which once set in motion has to be maintained.

So just as the question arises as to whether it is possible for the church to continue serving such demands when such heavy pressures are put on the small committed group, the question also arises as to whether the church should be prepared to take on new demands. Should it set up new structures (as it did in response to the needs of the past) to satisfy new needs, and so possibly fall into the same trap again, or is there another way of approaching the commitment to serve? Perhaps rather than using specific structures set up by the church, individual Christians should be free to move into areas of life where they could be available to stand beside those in need. Then identification, erosion and emancipation would take place within the framework of the individual Christian's life, using the existing structures in society, and causing more relevant ones to be built. This would mean that individual Christians would work as yeast and salt within society; trying to change its structures, and its behaviour. Yet they would not be burdened by the responsibility of administering and maintaining the overheads for such work (except in particular situations that would be the exception rather than the rule).

Support for the idea that it should be the individual lives of Christians rather than the structure of the church that should express the church's service to those in need, comes from another, rather unexpected quarter. Julius Nyerere, President of a young underdeveloped country where the Christian churches have done a great deal in the past for the development of educational, medical and agricultural facilities, and himself a practising Christian, has considerable experience of Christian service. He feels strongly that the churches should no longer run their own educational and medical structures. He would rather see the same amount of Christian commitment in the form of individual Christians working within the existing Government structures.

He advocates this because he thinks that then it would be seen by others as Christian service with no strings attached. For while the church runs its own structures such service can be interpreted as a bribe to encourage unbelievers into the faith, or as a way in which it can still have control over people's lives and their development: 'By separating the provision of service from its evangelical activities the Church will make it clear that it desires men's conversion to Christianity to come from conviction, not from gratitude or from the compulsion of indebtedness.' (*Freedom and Development*, p. 221). Such a statement is a real challenge to the church and its commitment to serve those in need. So often in the past the service has been done knowing that such contact will help in evangelism. For Christians to serve as individuals, purely for the sake of serving, and without anticipated gain might be more costly in terms of involvement, but it might also show that Christians are prepared to serve others disinterestedly. Incidentally it would also free the church from the structure organisation that so often distracts it from its primary function.

A Christian is a member both of the local church and of the Kingdom of God; his membership of the church must be taken seriously and not crowded out, but his Christian principles have to be worked out with secular society. Obviously, service to those in need is too complicated to be purely an individual matter. There will be times when corporate actions and structures will be required; when available structures in society will be inadequate for the job in hand. It may then be necessary for the church to act as a corporate body. It may also have to act corporately in denouncing a particularly pernicious evil. Yet, at the same time, Nyerere's assessment, although needing to be applied to our own situation, is a timely reminder that the church must not fall into the same trap twice, and impoverish her worshipping life by having to look after cumbersome structures that soon become irrelevant. This assessment will need to be considered very seriously when new patterns of ministry for the local church are being worked out.

Note

Jesus walked consciously towards the intense suffering and rejection of Calvary because he knew that through it alone would come the glory of the resurrection. Such a walk was the core of his commitment. Similarly he expects us to face and live with real suffering, deprivation, and rejection, so that the glory of the cross and resurrection may become manifest in our own lives, and to those with whom we live. Rather than avoiding deprivation through the accumulation of affluence, we are called to find Christ at the place where Christ is, i.e. with the hungry, the stranger, the naked, the sick, the prisoners (cf. Matthew 25).

CHAPTER SEVEN

The Meaning of Salvation and the Identity of the Church

If the church really changes its attitude towards oppression and injustice it will need to rethink completely its theology of mission, in evangelism and social involvement. What does the church mean by the salvation of man? What is salvation? The answers to such a question, if they are different from previous answers, will lead to changes in the identity of the church, as it goes about its task. It is in this theological area that I want to close this study. For it is essential for any practical stance to be theologically based. And if, as we have seen, our practical and theological position has been on shaky foundations in the past, it is all the more important to be sure that, when changing, we change to a firmer theological position. I will begin by considering two traditional positions that have strongly influenced the church's life; the individualistic and dualistic/evangelical approach and the corporate/holistic/radical approach. I shall then consider ways of eliminating some of the weaknesses within each of these positions, and suggest a more positive approach. These suggestions as to the meaning of salvation and the identity of the church will, hopefully, reflect the twofold frame of reference, the Bible and the experience of human existence, that has been the basis of our study so far.

1. The Evangelical Position

The main emphasis of this position has always been that the most important aspect of the Christian faith has been man's relationship to God – the vertical axis. Salvation is seen in terms of man's need to accept God. Man has sinned but Christ died as a substitute, giving up his life so that individuals can have new life through accepting his. Salvation is received by individuals who accept Christ's sacrifice in faith, and thus experience complete forgiveness and new life. This approach has led to a strong emphasis on 'soul winning', the main aim of the church being to go out and 'convert' people. Faith in Christ is seen as the answer to everything. Such faith is a personal matter and so these Christians express their faith in personal terms. Until recently there has been little appreciation of the corporate nature of faith, and so little awareness of social and structural sin. The answer to social evil is – more converts. Becoming a Christian is seen as the answer to all matters of morality. And although it is expected and assumed that a man's morals will change with his new found faith, so often that doesn't happen.

This theological position approaches faith and life in a dualistic rather than holistic manner. Underlying all attitudes, is the feeling that man is a divided being with a 'physical' side that relates to the fallen world and a 'spiritual' side that relates to God. This attitude can lead to a conflict as to which side is the more important. So far, the 'spiritual' side of man has held the ascendancy, so priority has always been given to evangelism in Christian Mission, and there is a more intellectual approach to faith. A man considers the faith, accepts it inwardly, and is then able to be at ease. Yet the response in terms of behaviour is not always forthcoming. The faith is understood in his mind yet not expressed in 'deed and truth'. Love can so easily be theoretical rather than practical, and people are perhaps seen as souls to win rather than as whole people. This interpretation creeps into the use of the Bible itself. 'The Word' is seen to be the guiding source of everything. Yet the practical implications of what it says are not regarded with the same awe as are the 'spiritual' sayings. This kind of dualism affects attitudes to the world, which is seen as both sacred and secular. Whatever is sacred is holy and according to God's ways. Whatever is secular is profane, and works against God's plan. The church (the body of Christians) is seen as holy, and therefore is the main (or possibly only) agent for bringing about God's will. The world is the sphere of the devil and is regarded with fear and contempt. There is only a grudging acceptance that God uses unbelieving secular society. Though God's world is seen as being intrinsically good, its fallen nature is strongly emphasised. So Christians are called to come out of the world, so as not to be tainted by it, and the church is seen as a guerilla organisation, fighting for a 'spiritual' cause in a 'physical' world which opposes it.

The ultimate goal is Heaven, where each individual Christian is at one with God, in a totally new society. Heaven is seen more in terms of a 'spiritual' otherworldly existence than a 'physical' reality emanating from God's original Creation. The hope of heaven is also seen as a panacea since there everything will be explained and oppression and injustice, pain and suffering will come to an end. Therefore we are encouraged not to worry too much about the problems of the present, for they will all be answered on the Day of Judgement.

Such a theological position has obviously affected attitudes towards social action. There have, of course, been exceptions to the rule, as in the case of John Wesley and later the Victorian reformers, Shaftesbury, Wilberforce, and the Clapham Sect. The Salvation Army was a major force for social change and there have been many charitable organisations set up and much legal reform work done in the past two hundred years. However, as has been described by David Moberg (cf. *The Great Reversal*, pp. 28 ff), soon after the turn of the century there was a clear swing away from these developments (except in the overseas missionary work where concern for education and health was developed). The amount of social service declined, and the primary emphasis became the preaching of the Word. Recently, the debate between evangelism and social concern has re-emerged. But social involvement for the majority of evangelicals is often a matter of secondary importance, rather than a primary requirement of the Christian life.

Social involvement has also been used unscrupulously as a 'bait' for the 'gospel', a way to build bridges and communications with unbelievers, so that once the contact has been made, the 'spiritual' message can be got across. If such social involvement does not produce results, i.e. people 'being converted', then it is questioned.

It is true that there are a number moving forward from such attitudes, but it takes time for changes in traditional attitudes to percolate at a local church level. Most of the older members of those congregations will never really change from the pattern they have grown up with.

2. The Radical Position

The radical position has placed more emphasis on the importance of man's relationship to man and making the best use of God's creation, in order to find God and true humanity at the same time. A radical thinks the sins that are most abhorrent to God are hatred, injustice, and divisive oppression. Structures can be even more effec-

THE MEANING OF SALVATION

tive purveyors of injustice than individuals. To the radical, salvation is being set free to be human, and to realise one's God-given potential. It means being free from injustice, oppression, greed, deprivation. Salvation, as Gutierrez puts it (*A Theology of Liberation*, pp. 150-2), is more concerned about a 'qualitative and intensive' approach rather than a 'quantitative and extensive' one. It is more concerned about 'the value of human existence' than it is about 'the number of persons saved, the possibility of being saved, and the role which the Church plays in the process'. This leads to a more universal approach where 'man is saved if he opens himself to God and to others, even if he is not clearly aware that he is doing so. This is valid for Christians and non Christians alike, for all people.' Salvation is seen as 'something which embraces all human reality, transforms it, and leads it to its fullness in Christ. Thus the centre of God's salvific design is Jesus Christ, who by his death and resurrection makes it possible for man to reach fulfilment as a human being. This fulfilment embraces every aspect of humanity; mind and body, individual and society, person and cosmos, time and eternity. Christ the image of the Father, and the perfect God Man, takes on all the dimensions of human existence.' (Working Draft of the Medellin Conference in *Between Honesty and Hope*, p. 189 – quoted by Gutierrez.) Salvation becomes a universal experience, whereby God works within people and their relationships with each other, liberating them to become fully human and find their fulfilment in Christ. In biblical terms this liberation is seen clearly in the Exodus, where God acts to free his people to become themselves. There, the community is freed to inaugurate a new qualitative society, that will speak to the rest of the world of God's fulness for man.

So it can be inferred that salvation, in the radical sense, has a different end from that of evangelical interpretation; salvation happens in the here and now, in distinct historical situations, whenever man becomes more 'human'. Indeed as Gutierrez puts it (*ibid.*, p. 160): 'Building a just, peaceful, and fraternal, human society is what salvation is all about.' In liberation from oppression and re-enaction of the Exodus theme in today's world, God's salvation is being revealed to the world at large. With this emphasis on the present effect of salvation, the future effect is less clear. There are some radicals who emphasise that the future is open-ended, completely dependent on what happens in the present. There is no idea of an intervention by God to establish his kingdom. The future exists only 'to the extent that there is hope', that 'can only emerge from now, from one's commitment to historical praxis'. So as well as emphasising man's relationship to man, radicals also see the present as being crucial to Christian existence. Certainly there is no room for rest in this world, knowing that everything will be rosy after Judgement Day. There is seen to be only one history of the world. As Gutierrez puts it: 'There are not two histories one profane, and one sacred, juxtaposed or closely linked. Rather there is only one human destiny, irreversably assumed by Christ, the Lord of history. His redemptive work embraces all the dimensions of existence, and brings them to their fullness' (*op. cit.* p. 153). Existence is whole, and Christ speaks to that whole, so there is no conflict between man's spiritual and physical needs. He too is whole.

There are radicals who do not conceive of any supernatural power, such as the Holy Spirit, intervening from outside events to effect God's plan within the world. God and his salvation are made known to us through Christ 'Since God has become man, humanity, every man, history, is the living temple of God' (Gutierrez – *Theology of Liberation*, p. 194). So there is no sacred power that comes to work in profane man to reveal God to man; for man in his wholeness is already aware of Christ through his neighbour. As we come to know our neighbour, we become automatically aware of the incarnate Christ and hence the fullness of his salvation.

3. Areas of Interaction

Over the past ten years different emphases in Christian thinking have sometimes interacted, hardening attitudes towards the meaning of salvation rather than bringing them together. However, there has been a deeper mutual understanding of the problem itself.

The issue came to a head at the W.C.C. Meeting at Uppsala in 1968 with clear confrontation. Some of the pre-conference material angered the evangelicals because of the assertion that salvation was going to be dealt with only in its wider political and social aspects. 'We have lifted up humanisation as the goal of mission.' Humanisation was to be seen as the main driving force of evangelism and salvation. Arthur Glasser called the conference a 'watershed in relations between conservative evangelicals and liberals'. 'The focus of their polarisation was the essence of the Gospel, and its relation to the urgent task of human development.' ('Salvation Today and the Kingdom' in McGavran ... *Missions Tomorrow*, p. 33.) He claimed that the evangelicals were appalled with the 'secularised gospel and the reduction of the mission of the Church to social and political activism'. The result was that when the draft statement on this issue came to the floor of the conference to be approved, it was sent back for further revision. The end result was, of course, so ambiguous that it satisfied no one. So the confrontation had raised the issue, but had not been able to resolve it; indeed there was hardly even an understanding of one side's claims by the other.

After the conference, the Report was issued for discussion, and the debate continued. A strong conservative 'evangelical' response came in the Frankfurt Declaration, 1970, which was aimed at refuting what lay behind the Uppsala Report: the radical theology of humanisation. In particular, it was concerned with which 'frames of reference' were important when considering the meaning of salvation. The primary frame of reference in any discussion of salvation was thought to be the Bible, and it was implied that the situation of human encounter was therefore secondary. Thus Peter Beyerhaus, a leading figure in the Frankfurt Declaration, argued that mission therefore occurs '*primarily* in the proclamation of the redemptive act of Jesus Christ's kingly lordship'. He then went on to say that 'It is *accompanied* by the authenticating presence of the new life in the Spirit within the community of the Church, by the transforming power of the Spirit in believers, also in their obedient attempts to bring about social changes' (*Missions Which Way? Humanisation or Redemption*, p. 68). He reiterates this later: 'the planting and growth of the Church as the body of Christ in the world remains the *primary* goal of mission within history. The transformation of this world is the *result* of a membership which is prepared to serve', (*ibid.*, p. 69). He puts evangelism before social action; man's social state is seen to be the concern of Christians who have already responded to the gospel, rather than being a concern of the gospel itself. This approach has been the basis of the evangelical response, right up until the debate after the Lausanne Conference, with the preaching of the Word remaining primary, and social action secondary.

After Uppsala came the conference in Bangkok in 1973 under the title 'Salvation Today'. Both sides of the argument were fully represented at the conference, and there were high hopes that some definite conclusion might be reached as to the meaning of salvation today. But, although matters became clearer than at Uppsala, no definitive statement was made. However, from the evangelical point of view, a step forward was taken, in that it was at least acknowledged that there was a personal aspect to salvation, as well as a social and political aspect. Christ's salvation was seen as the 'salvation of the soul and body, of the individual and society, mankind and the groaning creation' (Report from Sect. 2, Salvation and Social Justice. *World Conference on Salvation Today*. See Bangkok Assembly, 1973, p. 38).

Where can I a copy of the Lausanne Covenant?

Then came the Lausanne Conference on Evangelism in 1974, the W.C.C. Assembly at Nairobi in 1975, and the National Evangelical Anglican Conference, 1977, where the ferment continued. The Lausanne Covenant affirmed for evangelicals the primacy of evangelism over social action (Sect. 6, Lausanne Covenant) and denied any sense that evangelism could be seen as social action or political liberation (Sect. 5). At the same time concern for a deeper social involvement has continued to grow.

However, a change has appeared in the evangelical position, even at the theological level, in a number of books on the subject and at N.E.A.C. 77. Richard Mouw, in describing the meaning of salvation, moves far closer to the radical, holistic view, when he says that Jesus came to save 'the entire created order from the pervasive power of sin' (*Political Evangelism*, p. 13). He clearly accepts that salvation refers to a wider area of life than some evangelicals had previously accepted. And Orlando Costas also emphasises the need to recognise the cosmic significance of sin, and the need for an evangelistic answer, that is not aimed solely at the individual, but also at the whole structure of society. 'The scope of the evangelistic activity of the people of God must include the presentation of the fullness of the power of the gospel as it confronts the cosmic presence of sin in the created order. Political evangelism (i.e. political activity) then is one important aspect of this overall task of evangelism.' ('Evangelism and the Gospel of Salvation' in *International Review of Missions*, 1973, p. 31.) And in the statement from N.E.A.C. 77, there are hints of a similar attitude, even though it is carefully guarded. Section C 1 states 'Reconciliation to God implies a righting of all that is opposed to the Lordship of God. This includes physical healing, reform in social and political structures, and healing personal relationships.' So reconciliation is seen to have cosmic implications, even though the statement then goes on to question whether salvation can be thought of in this holistic way.

It is now being realised, that to appreciate what God's salvation is for the whole world order, it is necessary to appreciate all forms of evil and sin within that world order; be they personal, corporate or structural. Only when the extent of the influence of evil is appreciated, can the fullest understanding of God's salvation be reached.

4. Historical Context

It may now be helpful to put the debate into the context of earlier Christian attitudes. There has always been a part of the church which has stressed the importance of Jesus Christ the redeemer and

THE MEANING OF SALVATION 133

of the Bible, and another part which has stressed culture and society, God's creation, as being the most important factor influencing the way in which Christians express faith. Reinhold Niebuhr has described this confrontation in his book *Christ and Culture*. In it, he outlines three major approaches: firstly that of those who see Christ as being against culture, following 1 John, through Tertullian, Tolstoy, Wycliffe and modern extreme sectarian groups. Secondly, Christ is seen within culture, as in the Christian Gnostics, Abelard, and the Culture Protestantism of Ritschl. And thirdly Christ and culture are seen in synthesis (Aquinas), or in paradox (Luther), or Christ is seen as the Transformer of culture (Augustine, Calvin and F. D. Maurice). Today we are involved in the same discussion. There are still those who see Christ revealed in the Bible, speaking against the culture of our environment. There are still those who see God as speaking to man from society and its present day culture. And there are still those who see God as speaking both through Christ, divinely revealed through the Bible, and also through the present day expressions of human existence. The first view stresses redemption and man's fallen nature, emphasising the individual, and taking an 'exclusive' view of the Church which inclines towards a ghetto mentality. God is depended on as the one who is beyond and the Kingdom of God is regarded as belonging to a future which is discontinuous with the present. It is a dualistic approach. The second view stresses the Creation and Incarnation, with a corporate and social emphasis and a universalist attitude which leans toward acceptance of culture and an insistence on salvation in the here and now. The Kingdom is seen as continuous with the present. It is a holistic approach. And the third path seeks to hold these two views in tension whilst rejecting the weaknesses of both. It is to this third view that I incline, seeking to do justice to a twofold frame of reference; on the one hand there is the biblical revelation of Christ, and on the other every thing that speaks to us from our experience of human existence. This holistic view of salvation is what I am seeking to convey.

It is worth mentioning some recent thinking on this critical balance between Christ and culture that reminds us of the need to be aware of our own presuppositions. Dr. Norman, in his 1978 Reith Lectures, entered the debate by calling on present day political theologians to beware of the way theology is being influenced by contemporary political ideologies. 'The identification of Christianity with human rights ideology, in fact, is the contemporary manifestation of a permanent phenomenon: the adoption by the Church leadership in each successive generation of the moral and political idealism of the surrounding secular culture.' (*Reith Lecture*, No. 3 – 1978.) He endorses the view of that body of Christians who have always been wary of the influence of contemporary culture on Christian interpretation. Chris Sugden raises a similar point ('One Bible for the Rich?'–*Third Way*, October 1978) recognising that we all interpret the Bible according to our cultural conditioning, and he goes on to ask whether biblical interpretation should be more influenced by our own culture or by the culture of the time when the text was written.

Concern for the way in which Christian interpretation and expression is influenced by contemporary society has been central to this book. Faith has often been sidetracked by secular thought, and Christian thinking is now changing its allegiance from one side to the other – from being the handmaiden of the establishment, to being the spouse of the poor and oppressed. A closer affinity with the Marxist analysis is emerging as some Christians have been forced to realise that of the two major ideologies, Marxism is closer to the Christian faith than capitalism. But we cannot afford to attack the influence of past ideologies over Christianity only to be absorbed by new ideologies in the future. What is required is not further adaptation to secular ideologies but a biblical ideology that is both related to the society in which we live, and at the same time able to stand critically apart from it through its own dependence on the prophetic revelation of God's word.

It is the uniqueness, possessed by no other ideology, of the biblical revelation of God to man, that must dominate our understanding of mankind and our view of the Kingdom of God. We must not be overimpressed by the individualistic approach of capitalism, nor become satellites of the collectivist approach of Marxism. We must seek a corporate expression that is true to the Body of Christ, the church, as Jesus envisaged it, and also true to the intrinsic nature of the Kingdom of God, that seeks to draw all men together under the Lordship of Christ.

5. Holistic View

It is indeed difficult to do full justice both to the person of Jesus Christ, Son of God, revealed through the Bible, and also to our present human existence. In the past, all attempts to express one formula that does justice to both the divine and the human qualities of existence have foundered. It is so easy to explain salvation in terms of a personal encounter between man and God, or in terms of a transcendent change in relationships between man and man.

THE MEANING OF SALVATION

But what is required is an understanding of salvation that is true both to the divine nature of God and to the reality of human existence, one that is both personal and corporate, one that sees man as requiring salvation for all his needs as a whole person, rather than requiring salvation for certain aspects of life only. Salvation can then be interpreted in the light of both God's work of creation, and also his work of redemption. It is only when salvation can be understood in the light of both of these awe-inspiring gifts to humanity, that a Christian can feel he is expressing the meaning of the word adequately. So there can be no going back to a dualistic understanding of God and man, nor can there be a watering down either of God's divinity or man's highest potentiality.

J. Miguel Bonino (*Revolutionary Theology Comes of Age*, p. 165) describes mankind as placed within a threefold realm of responsibility. Man is seen as responsible to his fellow man, to nature (the cosmos) and to God himself. Therefore any understanding of salvation needs to include each of these three relationships. Firstly, man will need to see how salvation affects his relationships and responsibilities to all other men. Injustice towards others, whether structural or personal, domination that oppresses others and makes either groups or individuals less than human, behaviour that reduces the human potential of a person, division or discord between men, will need to be dealt with if salvation is to have any reality. Secondly, man will need to see how salvation affects his relationship with the world, the way he uses the world, and its natural resources. True salvation will not entertain misuse of such resources, or any unequal distribution of them. Salvation will not be satisfied with natural or potential resources being used for inadequate or unjust ends. It will expect such resources to be used towards the inauguration of God's purpose for this world. So any wrong relationship between man and God's creation will need to be changed if salvation is to have its full meaning. Thirdly, man will also need to understand how salvation affects his relationship with God himself. Any similar discord between man and God will need to be reconciled. Any failure of man to live up to God's standards will need to be remedied. Any inability of man to fulfil the plan that God has for him will need to be eliminated. Any inadequacy in bringing about the New Kingdom, the New Creation, God's sovereign will for the whole of humanity, and the whole of creation, will need to be overcome. Any unwillingness by man to recognise his dependence on, and his need to worship and obey, his Creator will need to be rectified. All these matters will require attention if salvation is to be understood fully in terms of human existence.

Before going any further, I shall give a practical example of the way salvation works on all of these three levels, whatever the issue. Take for instance the issue of justice. Brian Wren has pointed out, in his very helpful book, *Education for Justice* (pp. 43–55), that three different aspects can be detected in the overall biblical view of justice. The first aspect, he defines as natural justice, which concerns the equal value and dignity that is the right of every human being; i.e. 'that each person has a human right to the most extensive basic liberties compatible with a like liberty for all' (*op. cit.* p. 55). The second aspect, he defines as saving justice. This justice is expressed by God's commitment to stand beside those who have been oppressed, downtrodden and deprived. The best example of this is the Exodus, where God revealed himself historically, by showing he was committed to a justice that was concerned not only with the personal, but also with the political, social and economic spheres of life. The third aspect, he defines as loving justice. It is the attitude expressed by Jesus, which goes beyond the point of human justice. Whereas justice would condemn a man like Zacchaeus the unjust tax collector for extorting money unfairly from others, Jesus goes further in his meeting with Zacchaeus. He attempts to create justice by getting Zacchaeus to repent and repay the stolen money. This kind of justice is a 'love that surpasses justice in the hope that justice can at last be created' (*op. cit.* p. 51).

Now the first two forms of justice, natural and saving justice, can be seen to be concerned with salvation in terms of man's relationship with man, and with creation (i.e. the world's resources). They are concerned with the implementation of God's salvation with the aim of restoring to human existence the true humanity envisaged by God originally, whereas the third form of justice, loving justice, is more concerned with bringing back justice into man's relationship with God, (though that restoration may in turn result in a renewed commitment towards justice between man and man as well). It seeks to bring salvation into the heart of man, which is so cut off from God that it produces continual injustice. Therefore any understanding of justice would be inadequate if it stressed only natural or even saving justice, without appreciating the distinct significance of loving justice. It would also be inadequate if it expressed only loving justice, without realising that such justice leads on automatically to a commitment to both natural and saving justice. Full salvation therefore with regard to justice, needs to be expressed in all three areas; in man's relationship to man, to the world, to God.

When, therefore, man is able to relate to fellow man, nature, and God, in a satisfactory way, then he will have started to fulful his true humanity, and God's purpose and will for him. Then he will come to understand the full meaning of salvation, and also the true meaning of God's world. Salvation, then (to follow Bonino's theme), is not a step beyond humanity, as is so often thought, but a step towards it. In achieving salvation, man will become completely liberated from the shackles that inhibit so much of his present behaviour, and will be free to pursue his true human, God-given potential. And he will also come to see that such salvation brings that fullness of humanity only through the person of Jesus Christ who revealed the very being of God. It is only in the life, work, and witness of the God/man Jesus, that man will find the key to the meaning of salvation. For it is only Jesus who has been able to make clear the purpose of both the divine and the human in the life of the world.

i) *Humanisation and the Kingdom*

How in holistic terms is man's humanity to be understood? Here what is said by radicals about the humanisation of mankind has much to commend it. Bonino's words again state this overall perspective: 'Faith in Christ is not a step beyond humanity, but towards it.' We are looking for signs of true humanity within God's world, the humanity God envisaged. Those signs point the way to the structure of the New Kingdom. The way of Christ is not against what is truly human; it is only against the humanity that is tainted by sin. So just as Christ built his life on what was truly human so we are called to build on the humanity that God originally envisaged for man. On that basis Gutierrez's words ring true: 'Building a just, peaceful and fraternal human society is what salvation is all about' (*Theology of Liberation*, p. 160). For by 'just, peaceful and fraternal', we mean nothing other than the original purpose and plan that God had for human existence. Within this understanding of what true humanisation is, it does indeed become the goal of the Church's mission. Evangelism does become intricately involved with politics, and salvation can be seen as social justice. Surely what Jesus said at the synagogue in Nazareth speaks to us afresh: 'The Spirit of the Lord is upon me, because he has anointed me to preach good news to the poor. He has sent me to proclaim release to the captives and recovering of sight to the blind, to set at liberty those who are oppressed, to proclaim the acceptable year of the Lord.' (Luke 4: 18–19.) What Jesus saw himself as called to do, so we are called to do also. As Orlando Costas has put it, 'Humanisation, understood in its biblical perspective, is not a merely indirect result of Christ's saving action, it is at the heart of Christ's redemptive activity, for Christ came to recreate fallen humanity' (*The Church and its Mission*, p. 195). So we are called to follow Christ's footsteps, and work with him in today's world, to recreate fallen humanity according to the original pattern of God.

This will clearly entail deep and bitter conflict. It involves standing against all forms of evil and sin within the world. It involves recognising the cosmic nature of evil, and working for its total overthrow; the task indeed of the Kingdom. It involves appreciating the depth of evil within man, in his relations with other men, and with the world itself. It also means appreciating the evil that breaks man's relationship with God. It involves recognising evil at the personal level as well as at the structural level in society. It involves a continual battle with that evil, until it is cast out at the coming of the Kingdom of God.

This then is the task of the follower of Christ, and of the church. For the church's life is set in this battle. It is set within the already inaugurated, yet still incomplete, Kingdom of God. It is called to work and stand for the coming of the Kingdom in history. This means it dare not be a 'ghetto' church, retreating into itself, afraid of the world around. On the contrary the church's 'only concern, is for the full responsibility of man, not the vindication of some restricted sphere of God' (*Revolutionary Theology Come of Age*, p. 168). The church cannot afford to be unsure of God's ability to conquer evil within the world. It must recognise that its place is there, in the forefront of the historical and cosmic battle, being an agent in God's plan to restore humanity to its proper allegiance, which is to the Kingdom of God. It must realise that any form of dualist understanding of a 'holy' area, and a 'profane' area within humanity, is an insult to God's overall power and purpose. For God is at work throughout his creation, working for the ultimate fulfilment of the Kingdom inaugurated by Christ, and the total humanisation of man. That is the purpose of God's creation.

ii) *True Divinity*

Salvation, however, is not just concerned with a return to man's true, God given, humanity. It is also concerned with all the intrinsic qualities of God himself. It is those qualities that we must now seek to express if we are to appreciate the fullness of the salvation God offers to man. So far we have spoken of God's personality through the idiom of the created world, and of man as he has been created in his image. However, in the Christian faith there is another way in which God reveals himself to man. He has revealed himself to us through scripture, through his Word to us, and through the historical person of his Son, Jesus Christ. And it is this revelation that we must take note of if we are to come to the fullest understanding of God's being. For, to see God purely in terms of how we see him through man and creation, makes our belief purely subjective; whereas the Christian faith, since the coming of Christ on earth, is not merely subjective but is based on objective historical fact as well. And whereas, if we are not careful, belief based on our understanding God, through looking at man and creation, can lead towards humanism; by looking instead to the historical expression of God's being, as presented in the life, death and resurrection of Jesus, we can avoid the danger of humanism and be led to understand God's true being, rather than just the personal picture we have in our minds. We must then, of necessity, go back to the Bible. By looking at God's activity as it is described in the Old Testament, by studying his word spoken by prophet, psalmist, historian, priest and king, we can begin to appreciate the values he upholds, and the evil he condemns. By following the actions and teaching of Jesus, we can discover God's assessment of the present state of humanity, and what he offers as an answer to man's predicament. By studying the New Testament Christian response we can appreciate God's offer of a way out.

Jesus had a distinctive attitude towards evil and throughout his ministry was in no doubt about the depth and consequences of evil in the world. He refused to compromise in any way with it. The account of the temptations in the wilderness is evidence of this. He became aware of the presence of evil, of its persistence, and the temptation to compromise. Yet he fought it to the death, the ultimate result of his refusal to compromise. We are called today to make a similar assessment of the evil that is deeply ingrained within individuals and structures; of its persistence despite mankind's development and of the temptation we face to compromise. We are also called to make the same uncompromising stand against it and that will result in a fight to the death. Therefore we shall need to be on guard against compromise when we seek to act in our society. It is one thing to search for the humanisation of our society, but quite another to compromise with situations that in God's eyes are actually dehumanising. We cannot afford, therefore, to underestimate the presence and the power of evil around us, just as we must recognise the potential and worth of man as God has made him. And we need constantly to return to the values and standards exhibited by God, in the revelation given by Jesus Christ, and the scriptures. This will enable us continually to assess the influence of evil, and the poential for the Kingdom, within our own experience. Without God's standard of judgement, that can best be given to us through the past and present knowledge of Jesus Christ, we will fail to grasp what is essentially 'of the Kingdom' and what is 'of evil'.

Victory over evil depends on God's intervention, in Jesus Christ to initiate the victory, and in the Holy Spirit to implement the victory. The Holy Spirit is a real force in continuing the ministry and mediation of Jesus Christ himself. Without an appreciation of this Spirit, which is an expression of the divine being and his intervention in human existence, there can be no true understanding of the salvation that shatters the domination of humanity by evil and inaugurates the new Kingdom of God. In no way does the Holy Spirit deny the full humanity of man by coming to his aid in this way. On the contrary he enables man to become fully human, by becoming available. Man is still called to be man but he is also called to recognise his Creator. As Orlando Costas puts it 'Thus man is co-worker but God still remains THE WORKER. Without his sustaining grace man cannot function' (*op. cit.* p. 257).

iii) *The Future*

Jesus in his ministry shows also a distinctive view about the divine and human timescale. He was very aware that his ministry was to inaugurate the Kingdom of God; yet at the same time he knew that the final and total expression of the Kingdom was yet to come. The Kingdom therefore was both in the present and in the future. It was to be continuous with what was already inaugurated; and yet in another way it was to be discontinuous, separate, and different from present human existence. It is clear that any emphasis that presents the Kingdom, mainly as a heavenly state, in a future that is discontinuous with the present is an inadequate interpretation of what God's salvation is, for the fullness of humanity. Yet at the same time, to see the Kingdom developing solely in the present, emerging out of the conflict between Christian understanding and society, continuous with what already exists, is equally a caricature and a devaluation. The final Kingdom will express far more of God's divine existence than we can comprehend from our finite position. To say that the Kingdom is, as Assman puts it, 'a horizon open before us' (*Oppression and Liberation, A Challenge to Christians*, p. 154) or 'that which keeps the future open; full of new possibilities' (Gutierrez), or the hope that 'arises out of the struggles of the present', is to leave a picture of the Kingdom that is far too earthly orientated to express a state that manifests, above all, a divine presence, that transcends our present human existence. Biblical salvation envisages a Kingdom that beginning from our humanity leads us into experiencing aspects of existence at present beyond our comprehension; a paradox expressed in the idea of the resurrection of our bodies. The new earth will be a continuous development of the creation, yet it will also express the new and final state that will unite us totally with the very being of God himself.

iv) *Christianity Identity*

So where then does a Christian find an identity that is distinctly different that both proclaims and serves? Such an identity will need to mark the person out clearly as a discipline and witness of Jesus Christ and at the same time it will show him to be a person dedicated to serving and helping man find his true humanity. It is in the expression of these ideas in practice that a true Christian identity lies. So let us look at how we can express such an identity.

Bonino has suggested (*op. cit.* pp. 70–171) that there is distinction between the explicit reference to Christ and an implicit reference to Christ. When Christians meet together as a corporate body to confess, to worship, to proclaim, they make explicit reference to the name of Christ, and are thus, by this expression, able to see themselves as being different from all others who are committed, perhaps for different reasons, to the task of humanising mankind. But when Christians serve, they are making their stand implicitly.

The interweaving of both explicit and implicit reference to one's faith would present a commitment that was both total, and challenging. Each would be an intrinsic part of a total expression of faith, and would need to be integrated together so that service so easily became worship itelf, with the body as much as the individual combining to serve as much as to confess and proclaim. The necessity of interaction between the two roles is further emphasised by O. Costas (*op. cit.* pp. 249–50). He says that to come to know salvation in Christ, to become part of his corporate body, is 'not so much a prize won as a responsibility given'. To know what it means to be free leads to a total commitment to serve with others, until they are free. This expects the corporate body of Christ to proclaim his name explicitly as its *raison d'être*, and yet at the same time be totally committed to serve humanity. Jurgen Moltmann offers a different variation on the same theme of Christian identity when describing the identity of the church. He mentions two aspects of Jesus' teaching to his disciples that are both very different and yet are part of the whole. In Matthew 25, the Judge says to the people on the right, 'Whenever you did this for one of the least important of these brothers of mine, you did it to me'. In John 20 he commissions his disciples: 'As the Father sent me so I send you.' From these two aspects Moltmann constructs an overall view of Christian identity. 'What is the true Church? The true Church is where Christ is. Christ is present in the mission of the believers, *and* the suffering of the "least of these". His community is therefore the brotherhood of the believers and the poor, the lovers and the imprisoned, the hopers and the sick. The apostolate says *what* the Church is, the "least of these" say *where* the Church belongs. Only if the Church realises in itself this double brotherhood of Christ does it really live in the presence of the crucified and exalted Christ' (*The Open Church*, p. 105, quoting from Benoit Dumas).

v) *The Church as Signbearer* [Trailblazer / Leader of the journey]

We have seen earlier how total salvation involves the Christian faith working towards the full humanisation of man, restoring him to the image given to him originally by God. The major task of the church, the Christian corporate body, is to be a signbearer to humanity, showing the way towards total humanisation, and the new Kingdom.

However important the church may be, it is not an end in itself but a means by which God's original plan for his creation can be recovered. Salvation is concerned, not with the church as such, but with the fulfilment of God's overall design.

At present, the church is so sadly lacking in the qualities of real salvation, that it can hardly be described as a signbearer to the Kingdom. (Maybe that is why some have looked elsewhere for more effective signs of the Kingdom and of salvation.) But even so, these are what the church ought to exhibit, here is the way of life it should follow if it is to be true to its Founder. 'What a difference it would make if national churches, local congregations ... instead of producing lopsided congregations subjugated to the status quo and engaged in the proclamation of salvation as a ticket to heaven, would plant liberated communities of believers who relate the claims and demands of the more just and humane society.' (*The Church and Its Mission*, p. 250.) If only this were to happen, the church would be seen to be the signbearer/covenant community, and mankind would begin to take more note of what it said, and of Christ's offer of salvation.